ANGELS FLY BECAUSE THEY TAKE THEMSELVES LIGHTLY

Other titles from Leicester Bay Books
by Robert Kirby and Pat Bagley:

Sunday of the Living Dead
Wake Me for the Resurrections
Pat and Kirby Go To Hell
Family Home Screaming
Kirby Soup for the Soul

Other titles by Robert Kirby:

Dark Angel -- Historical Fiction
Brigham's Bees – a novel

Other titles by Pat Bagley:

I Spy A Nephite
Norman The Nephite
and the A-Maze-ing Conference Center
Utah Survival Guide
Dinosaurs of Utah and Dino Destinations
This Is The Place!
Mormons: History, Culture Beliefs
J. Golden Kimball Stories Vol. 1
MORE J. Golden Kimball Stories Vol. 2

WAKE ME FOR THE RESURRECTION

ANOTHER COLLECTION OF MORMON ESSAYS AND CARTOONS BY THE SALT LAKE TRIBUNE'S

ROBERT KIRBY
AND
PAT BAGLEY

Salt Lake City

Wake Me For The Resurrection

Printed in the United States

Library of Congress Cataloguing-in-Publication Data
Kirby, Robert – 1953-
Wake Me For The Resurrection / by Robert Kirby; illustrated by Pat Bagley
p. cm.
Collection of articles written by the author in his religion section of the Salt Lake Tribune.
ISBN -- 978-1481898201 (softcover)
1. Mormons—Anecdotes I. Title
BX8638.K57 1996
289.3'79258—dc20 96-43697
CIP

Leicester Bay Books
3877 Leicester Bay South Jordan UT 84095
www.leicesterbaybooks.com

First Edition by Buckaroo Books: 1996 --
ISBN -- 1 -885628-47-1 (OOP)
Second Edition by Leicester Bay Books (CS): 2013 --
ISBN -- 978-1481898201
Kindle Edition: 2013

Cover illustrations by Pat Bagley
Design by Richard Erickson & Pat Bagley

Book Two in the Collection of Mormon Humor series with
Sunday of the Living Dead
Pat & Kirby Go To Hell
Family Home Screaming
Kirby Soup for the Soul

This book is dedicated to anyone who has been forced to seriously consider the possibility that Larry, Moe and Curley were the Three Nephites.

NO DOUBT – by now modern medical science can offer clinical evidence in support of the beneficial effects of a good belly laugh. Somewhere there must be an article in a medical journal documenting how laughter releases endorphins, which cause a chemical reaction resulting in the experience we interpret as pleasure or joy or just plain feeling good. Try it for yourself some afternoon on a bad day. And if you need a little help generating a chuckle, crack open *Wake Me For The Resurrection* while the boss (of the bishop) isn't looking.

Yes, Brother Kirby (with Pat Bagley firmly in tow) is back with another collection of 'best of' selections from his columns in the Salt Lake Tribune. In his latest effort to help us all become more comfortable with our Moism (see page 11), Kirby ponders the Mormon penchant for meetings, the peculiar plight of Gentiles in Utah, Mormon fashion, Christian tolerance, and zucchini. His conclusion: "The truth is that Mormons ARE weird…[But] anyone who thinks Mormons are the weirdest bunch of people they've ever seen doesn't get around much."

Robert Kirby's humor comes with no curative guarantees, but it does offer perspective. Kirby is one of us, foibles, follies, fat cells, and all. He might not always be right—but recognizing tat could be the first step in realizing that neither are we.

-- the publisher

Acknowledgements

No book is ever a solitary effort. As such the author and illustrator gratefully acknowledge the contributions made by millions of faithful but neurotic Latter-day Saints: in particular, seminary teachers, missionary companions, ward ball teammates, visiting teachers, scoutmasters, high council speakers, Sunday School teachers, and last but not least, Johnny Lingo.

Contents

KNOW YOUR MO

I dropped into a pub the other night. Oh, shut up, I was with friends. Besides, in case you haven't noticed, practicing Mormons make excellent designated drivers.

Anyway, I was minding my own business when someone came up and asked, "Hey, aren't you that Mo writer for the Trib?"

I punched him. He had it coming. This is the age where daring to be different is okay so long as nobody gets rude enough to notice. If he had called me a near-sighted Caucasian, I might have filed a class action lawsuit against him, too.

OK, truth is that being called a Mo isn't so bad. While it's not exactly a term of endearment, Mo beats some of the other things I've been called -- lots of them by fellow Mos.

To ease the tension between Mos and gentiles, I've come up with a brief Mo lexicon. Practice them. Learn to be comfortable with your Moism.

MO -- Mormon.

NO MO -- Non Mormon.

NO MO' MO -- Ex-Mormon.

MO NOPOLY -- Utah.

MO TOWN -- Provo.

MO PEDS -- People walking across the street to Temple Square and the Missionary Training Center in Provo.

MO HAIR -- Missionary grooming standards.

MO BILE -- Substance produced in LDS church leaders by Sunstone and Dialogue.

PO' MO -- Financially challenged Mormon.

MO JO -- Doors lead singer Jim Morrison after his baptism for the dead.

MO LASSES -- Mormon babes.

MO TEL -- Bishop's interview, tithing settlement, church court, etc.

MO CHA -- Acceptable LDS alternative to coffee. Postum, sometimes diet Coke.

SU MO -- Graduate of BYU law school.

MO GUL -- Large white Utah bird frequently seen in church history books, parking lots and dumps.

MO RALLY -- Third quarter BYU drive against the University of Utah.

MO SEY -- LDS sense of time. See also Mo-tion.

LOCO MO TION -- Post-game exodus from Cougar Stadium.

MO LESTERS -- Visiting and home teachers who drop by without calling first.

MO NOGAMY -- LDS marriage practices no matter how they're actually defined or structured.

MO MOW -- Cutting the grass at Temple Square.

MO TIF -- Two or more Mormons engaged in a loud difference of opinion.

MO MENT -- What LDS church officials intended to say regardless of what was actually said.

MO LD -- Elderly Mormon, temple worker, etc.

MO ANING -- LDS practice of bearing witness.

That's enough. The point of this is to take the sting out of being referred to as a Mo. It's important to remember that the word Mo can't technically be considered a derogatory word in Utah, parts of Idaho, Arizona and California, because there are so many Mos. Being called a Mo in no way gives Mos the right to respond with actual ACLU-certified racial, gender or religious slurs. Hurling insults is bad. Remember -- it ain't Mo to throw.

MORMON WHINE CELLAR

This year, my wife and I were invited to a mostly non-Mormon New Year's Eve party. Everyone at the party was drinking wine. It soon became apparent that we were out of our league. Not because we weren't drinking, but rather because we couldn't understand a word of what was being said.

People sat around sipping and talking about various wines, using big words like "bouquet" and "intriguing" and "&@#*! state liquor commission." They held forth passionately about a wine having nose and legs, whether it was dry or sweet. Meanwhile, the wife and I sat there feeling like the Clampetts.

I have a little experience with wine and so I'm not completely naive. Way back when I dared drink it, wine had all the palate attraction of a warm glass of Goofy Grape mixed with kerosene. Even if it wasn't against the Word of Wisdom, I wouldn't pour it on my neighbor's dog much less in my own stomach.

Although Mormons are supposed to steer clear of alcohol, there's no reason why we can't be equally proud of what we drink. There's a place for us in the world of liquid snobbery.

Toward that end, I've drawn up a Mo "wine list." You might want to clip this column and save it. Chances are that sooner or later you'll be invited to a Mormon do. A quick peek at it will save you from feeling and acting like a clod.

CHAMPAGNE DE ROOTE -- A heady little Mo number, perfect for swilling before, during or after meals. Frequently homemade in private Mo cellars by combining 60 pounds of sugar with a gallon of water, extract and dry ice.

SPUMANTE DI TUBER -- A commercial version of the above. Authoritative with just a touch of smart Bohemian class. You can't go wrong asking for a Hires '96 (July) or even a carafe of Vendage A&W.

Caution: these beverages are brisk enough to produce stupefying belches in the unwary. When taken a la mode, they both have the legs of an East German swimmer.

CHATEAU POONCH -- Direct from the cellars of BYU Food Service come two popular ward house numbers. Whether red or blue, the Chateau poonches are perfect haute refreshments for firesides, wedding receptions and missionary farewells.

Note: In Utah County, the red is known by less sophisticated celebrants as "red tongue" while the blue goes by the unfortunate nom de cultural hall of "Smurf piss."

AIDE DE KOOL -- Those requiring a broader experience in Mormon liquid culture will no doubt find exactly what they're looking for in a stunning array of packet beverages. Running the gamut from punishingly dry to nauseatingly sweet, (depending on how much sugar you add), these are perfect compliments to any potluck meal.

The clear but seductive green and yellow Kool are best with casseroles, while the heavier more firm red and purple Kools go better with cookies and cakes. Pork and beans call for a distinctive blue Googleberry. For a brisk spumante, add Sparkle, Sprite or Seven-up to taste.

LE MON DU AIDE -- Made from lemons, this popular refreshment is perfect for late afternoons. When made with insufficient sugar, it is neither intriguing nor supple but rather contains enough explosive authority to collapse your head.

WATER -- If you're a teetotaler, not to worry. Commonly served at most Mormon functions are several brands of waters, including Perrier au Tap and the less expensive but equally delightful Cascade de Jardin Hose.

Cheers. Maybe.

BORN TO BE BAD

Christians of all denominations come together on at least a one point; that the betrayal of Jesus in the New Testament was a pretty bad thing. Wherever he is right now, the general consensus among Christians is that Judas isn't having a very good time.

But what if betraying the savior of the world wasn't entirely Judas' fault? What if Judas just had it in his genes to be a traitor?

This is a fair question in light of the fact that scientists are so busy these days identifying the genes that make us tick. Scientists now say they've discovered a gene that could influence how excitable and impulsive a person might be.

An Associated Press story on the discovery claimed that people who ranked high in this new gene are above average when it comes to "novelty-seeking." They're "impulsive fickle, excitable, quick-tempered and extravagant, while those scoring below average tend to be reflective, rigid, loyal, stoic, slow to anger and frugal."

Hmm, that sounds exactly like the difference between people who go to church and people who don't.

Lets break this down, shall we? I'm thinking that maybe sinners have a lot of this new gene and saints don't. After all, it probably wouldn't be fair to say that Mother Teresa is quick-tempered, fickle and extravagant. Likewise, it's a safe bet that Genghis Kahn wasn't frugal and slow to anger.

Perhaps a more scientific test is in order. Choose the person you think has too many of these "novelty-seeking" genes.

A. Billy Graham
B. Pope John Paul
C. Kathy Lee Gifford
D. Judas Iscariot

The answer, of course, is C -- Kathy Lee Gifford. It can't be D because Judas is technically dead. This was a trick question, and, frankly, it's a bit disappointing to see that you weren't on your toes.

Hopefully, though, you see what I'm driving at. Like Gifford, Judas and probably you, most of my sins are the result of this gene making me excited and impulsive. So, if scientists are looking for a name for this new gene, they might want to call it the "sin gene."

Having a sin gene means that you can't go around saying "the devil made me do it" anymore. Mainly because scientists are fast proving that he didn't. The good news is that your genes made you do it and we've got lawyers in southern California today that can work miracles with stuff like that for a defense.

No, don't offer me any money or the Nobel Prize. I'm just glad I found another possible way of dodging damnation. It's a relief to know that the things which have brought so much condemnation, disapproval and police in my life have been the result of something far beyond my clumsy attempts to choose between right and wrong.

I've got this sneaking hunch that God, being a known disrespector of excuses, probably regards the sin gene the same way he regards Cuban cigars, bikinis, easy money, creative lying, voting Republican and being mean to cats. Namely that it's just another of life's temptations or hurdles that should be dealt with rather than indulged in.

It's kind of a bummer, though. I was waiting for scientists to discover the next gene. The most spiritual gene there is, the one that makes you sleep in church so you don't have to worry about guilt in the first place.

THERE IS NO DAMN IN RAMADAN

In case you've been too busy doing your home teaching, I'm going to point out that we're smack in the middle of something called Ramadan. If the first thing that popped into your mind is "What the heck kind of casserole is that?" you've been living in Utah too long.

Ramadan is actually a Muslim holy time. And if that makes you want to run right out and buy a metal detector, you don't know Muslims very well either. You're obviously confusing the two different kinds of Muslims.

The first kind of Muslim is the more sedate and peaceful Normal Muslims, of which there are slightly more or less than 1.5 billion. Then there are the fanatical and foul-tempered News Media Muslims, which number way less but who get all the press.

I've been a victim of the News Media Muslims before. When Ayatollah Khomeini died, I watched news clips from Iran of his funeral. The people there were so wrought up over the prophet being dead that they rioted, tearing open his coffin and crowd-surfing his corpse around like a scene out of a Van Halen concert. It was scary.

Most Utahns, indeed most Americans, think all Muslims are like that, blood-kin to an AK-47-armed Yosemite Sam. Say the word Muslim or Islam and all we can think of are yammering terrorists driving around in cars full of stuff that goes boom.

NOTE: Mormons who have this unfavorable view of Muslims should know that this country thinks only slightly better of them. A 1993 poll showed that 33% of Americans disliked Mormons while 36% disliked Muslims. The fact that this poll was conducted right after the Trade Center bombing, when Muslim stock was falling about as fast as Yasser Arafat pushed off a minaret, should tell us

Mormons a thing or two. Namely that if Muslims are the Yosemite Sams of the religion scene, we just gotta be the Elmer Fudds.

Where was I? Oh yeah, the truth is that the vast majority of Muslims are a far cry from the Middle East looneys we see in the news. They are a hard-working, peace-loving people trying to live according to the dictates of their God, who, incidentally, never told them to treat their women bad or go around blowing people up.

The bad rap that Muslims get stems from the news media's idolatrous worship of a God called Ratings, and a corresponding fascination with Islamic fanatics. Frankly, every religion, including Orthodox Journalism, has their nut cases. How would these other religions fare if world opinion of them was based solely on the behavior of people like David Koresh, Tammy Faye, or Sam Donaldson?

Right now, Muslims are observing Ramadan, a month-long period of turning away from earthly pleasures in order to concentrate on spiritual matters. They fast each day from dawn until dark, making this the equivalent of a really, really long Mormon Fast Sunday. Each night during Ramadan, Muslims gather at their mosque in Salt Lake City to pray. Ramadan will end around Feb. 20 with an all-day feast.

Granted, there are only about 3,000 Muslims in Utah, but 1 out of 5 people in this world is a Muslim. And since the world is getting to be a smaller place, it would do everyone in Utah some good if we got to know each other a little better. What better time than Ramadan?

14th ARTICLE OF FAITH

Most Mormons are familiar with the 13 Articles of Faith. If 99 percent of us can't recite the Articles of Faith verbatim, we at least know that the church has them. The articles outline our beliefs. They're what make us Mo.

Each article starts out with "We believe" and goes on to explain a tenant of Mormon belief. For example, the first article says we believe in God, Jesus Christ and the Holy Ghost -- except, of course, when the University of Utah is ahead.

Other articles deal with the structure of the church, revelations, spiritual stuff, etc. One even says we believe in being subject to whichever form of government happens to be in charge at the time. This is a particularly handy article for missionaries laboring in places where said government might be a junta, a dictatorship, or just a sullen roadblock in a jungle.

Mormons do okay with the 13 Articles of Faith. Where we really shine, however, is with the 14th Article of Faith. Like the other 13, good ol' numero 14 deals with a fundamental precept of Mormon belief and behavior. Here it is:

14. We believe in meetings -- all that have been scheduled, all that are now scheduled, and we believe that there will yet be many more great and important meetings. We have endured many meetings and hope to be able to endure all meetings. If there is a meeting, we seek after it.

Outside of Congress or an L.A. murder trial, nobody is a bigger fan of meetings than your average Mormon. We love meetings. Done right, you can get a serious buzz off of meeting boredom. Best of all, meetings aren't against the Word of Wisdom.

My own church job requires that I sit through 5-8 hours of meetings on any given Sunday. It works out to a butt-spraining eternity spent listening to stuff boring enough to be used as a rust preventative. Of this stuff, about three-quarters consists of stuff I've heard before, the rest of stuff I don't want to hear now.

Then there's the occasional church meeting during the week, a subtle program designed to ensure that I don't lose touch with the spirit of meeting during a week devoid of actual meetings. And apparently to make me hear more stuff.

Not all church meetings I go to are that bad. For the record, I won't even begin considering Sacrament meeting a waste of time unless it's a high council speaker or a Primary music program. All other meetings fall into varying degrees of useful purpose, some good, some falling so wide of actual constructiveness that they come down in neighboring galaxies.

There are three degrees of meetings in the LDS church. In order of importance (if not actual need) they are:

1. Worship. This category is restricted to Sacrament meeting, to which you gotta go if you wanna be Mo.

2. Work. This includes welfare, work projects and any other meeting where actual service is rendered to those in need.

3. Worthless. Any meeting held simply because the church handbook or some religious bureaucrat says it should be.

There is a fourth degree of meeting, Outer Meetingness, where participants meet with the sole (and brainless) objective of having a meeting. Approximately half of all church meetings fall into this category.

I have this theory --more of a personal article of faith, actually -- that Hell is just one big meeting.

RESERVED SEATING

Last Sunday, it occurred to me that I could tell who was in church and who wasn't just by looking at the spot where they normally sit. I discovered this while looking for my friend Ray Bradford.

Because it was only 10 minutes after the start of services, the customary Bradford family spot by the west doors was still empty. Although the chapel was full, people had still left the Bradford's a place to sit.

I looked around and saw that everyone else was in their usual spot. The Banjonecks were front and center where the bishop could see them. The Mutzes were midway on the left, the Snoots on the right. The Kirbys were clear in the very back, two of us playing a Game Boy.

Some people go to church with the idea that there's a seating plan. Sit in the spot they customarily occupy and it puts a serious strain on their Christianity. They'll spend the rest of the meeting staring at the back of your head, wondering where God got the nerve to create something as stupid as you.

There arc religions that have chapel seating plans. I went to church with a no Mo friend in South Carolina once. We sat in the same pew his family had been sitting in for almost 100 years. There was even a bronze plaque dedicating the pew to my friend's great-great grandfather. Seems gramps "bought" the pew back then by contributing a bunch of money to build the church.

Makes sense. My comparison, all I ever got for money contributed to my own church was about 40 church jobs and a couple of spaghetti dinners. It should be pointed out, however, that the boredom factor in both churches was exactly the same, a 9.5 on a scale of 1-10.

Mos don't have assigned seating in our chapels. It's first come, first flop. That we seldom have trouble is more a credit to our being creatures of sad habit than patience.

Actually, there are assigned seats in a Mo chapel. Three of them. You can sit in these seats, but it seriously disrupts the worship flow. They are (in reverse order of importance):

- The bishop's seat.
- The organist's bench.
- Wherever the bossiest woman in the entire ward and/or stake normally sits.

Sit in the bishop's spot and you could end up in charge of the ward. A bad thing by anyone's definition, but especially the bishop's wife's. Sit where the organist sits and you better be able to play something dirge-like.

You definitely don't want to sit in the spot where the ward's Alpha female normally parks her brood. If looks can kill, you won't even make the fourth Resurrection.

My favorite place to sit during church is the foyer. When I can't get a spot there, I generally take one inside the chapel but next to a door. I rarely get mad if someone else sits in my spots. I have, however, been known to cuff aside a deacon in order to get a seat.

Although it's not considered true worship by orthodox Mos, sitting in these obscure places accomplishes the same thing as sitting on the front pew in the chapel. I'm technically in church and I'm being reverent. Best of all, I've been doing it for so long that both the bishop and God know exactly where to find me if they need me.

AND WOMAN SAID...

I'm building a family room in my basement. Thus far, it's cost me three months, $5,000, a thumbnail, and every speck of my pride. I'll bet God didn't have this much trouble creating the world. Then again, maybe He did.

Christian theology holds with the belief that it took God six days to create the world. Six days means that God didn't just blink and the world was there. It means that the Creation was a process, going from A to B to C, etc.

Given that God is omnipotent, you'd think he could get from A to Z in under a minute. But the fact that it took Him six days suggests that someone else was involved, someone to whom the process and aesthetics were probably important. Someone like a woman.

People who build stuff know that women are very important in the creative process. One thing my family room taught me is that the image of whatever a man is creating changes in direct proportion to how hard the man has to work to get it. That, and not to get latex caulk in my ear ever again.

Because I was the one doing the work, it was therefore up to my wife to never lose sight of our original goal -- a comfortable family room with furniture and electrical outlets. Four weeks into the creation of our family room and I was ready to settle for milk crates and an extension cord.

Although it isn't in the Bible, when you stop and think of all the billions of picky things that went into the world, it pretty much stands to reason that God needed the help of a woman. Somebody had to remember why the world was getting built in the first place.

And Woman said: "You can't make parakeets eleven feet tall, for crying out loud. The PEOPLE are only five feet. And would you just look at Africa..."

I certainly made more mistakes building my family room than God made creating the world. Purists will, of course, argue that God is perfect and therefore technically incapable of making even a single mistake. But how else can you explain things like eggplant, Snoop Doggy Dog and the French government? I don't even try. Stuff like that makes my crooked door seem not so bad.

Besides, God made up for any possible production goofs by creating lightning, hot fudge, blue jeans, dogs, the Milky Way, Chris Isaak and hockey. Oh, and the '69 Boss 429 Mustang.

If I could know any creation secret in the universe, I wouldn't want to know how to make oceans or mountains. I'd like to know what God said when he missed a swing with a hammer and hit his thumb. When it happened to me, I said (deleted) and (deleted). I'm not saying God cussed, but it could explain all those Black Holes out there.

My favorite part of the Creation story is: "And on the seventh day God ended his work which he had made; and he rested on the seventh day from all his work which he had made." Hmm, a union job?

Unfortunately this is also the part of the Bible that suggests no women were involved in the Creation. From my experience, there's no way God would have gotten a day off.

And Woman said, "Hey, when are you going to finish the...?"

CARD CARRYING MORMON

Newcomers to Utah find a lot of Mormon stuff confusing. One of the things I've tried to do in this column is lower gentile-angst (if not actual gentile rage) by explaining this stuff. Today's topic is the Mormon temple recommend.

Most people know that Mormons build temples. It's what we do and we're pretty good at it, too. Temples are ultra-holy houses of worship. Only Mormons -- and not even a lot of us -- can go inside the temples. In order to do that, you've got to have a temple recommend.

A temple recommend is a small piece of paper about the size of a driver's license. You get it from your bishop and stake president by proving to their satisfaction that you've been behaving as a Mormon should. Your word usually suffices.

Technically, temple recommends are only good in the temple. In fact, outside of the Mormon Church, recommends are not considered an official document of any kind. Unlike an American Express card or a sturdy license, you can't even use them to scrape your windshield or jimmy a lock.

Temple recommends only have one use. Unfortunately, not everyone who has a recommend has figured this out.

For example, if a bartender cards you, it's considered a serious Utah social gaffe to show him your temple recommend. Not only are you not supposed to be drinking, but odds are he won't consider it a valid form of identification. Then again, he may buy you a drink for laughs.

Conniving business Mos will sometimes allude to possessing a temple recommend or even flash one in an effort to prove that they're trustworthy. When this happens, your moral and social obligation is to strike said person with something heavy and run away.

Back when I was a cop, people sometimes handed me their temple recommends when I asked them for ID. It didn't happen very often, say maybe five times in all the years I wore a badge. I never understood exactly why they did this unless it was to assure me that I wasn't dealing with a dirtbag. Didn't work.

One day, I stopped this guy for speeding. When I walked up to his window and asked for his driver license, he gave me his temple recommend, too. It bugged me so much that I wrote him a ticket, something I was going to do anyway. But then I got creative and wrote on the ticket that he was hereby disfellowshipped for exceeding the posted speed limit.

The guy didn't find this very funny and complained to my sergeant. I've still got a copy of the department's reprimand. It says, among other pointed things, that "your bizarre sense of humor and lack of professional restraint may prevent you from going far in law enforcement." Which, praise the Lord, turned out to be true.

Temple recommends aren't supposed to be flashed around like a Get-Out-of-Jail-Free card. Like most items of deep religious faith, having a recommend is supposed to be a personal thing.

Sadly, having a temple recommend can sometimes even work to your disadvantage. Some no-Mos think that any Mo who has one is suspect. They use the possession of a recommend to negatively stereotype Mormons, illogically believing that any Mo with a temple recommend is Ward Cleaver reincarnate. Actually, the truth is that even Eddie Haskell types like me have them.

I can't believe I just said that.

WASP vs. WORM

Despite the fact that most orthodox Mormons believe that change is a plan of Satan, change is actually good. Change is only bad if you're an inflexible, paranoid fuss-budget -- say about 49.6 percent of all active Mormons.

Mormons recently experienced a change that few will notice. There are now more Mos outside the United States than inside. Sometime last week, the balance of the church's population shifted subtly but inevitably to the non-WASP side.

Oops, I can't use WASP. It stands for "white Anglo-Saxon Protestant," and everyone knows that Mormons aren't Protestant. This social crisis calls for a new acronym reference to the typical Mo. How about BUGS, for "Born in Utah, Generic Saint?"

I've got a better one. WORM, for "white, orthodox, Republican Mormon." WORM isn't as snappy as WASP but a people comfortable with being the Lord's sheep shouldn't mind. What's more humble than a worm?

Where was I? Oh, yeah, the LDS church is gradually becoming less of a WORM organization. If things keep going this way, church is going to be a lot different than it is today.

The bad part is that noticeable change will still take about 900 years. It certainly won't happen fast enough to rattle the heads of anyone. It might be nice if it did. If we could compress time, say speed up the process of cultural change in the church to a few days instead of a century, it might shake up more of these mulish Mos.

Frankly, I'd like to see the Utah Mormon become a quaint figure in church history. Maybe then the stereo-typical Mo wouldn't be a WORM and simple-minded conformity would be less of a gospel issue than it is today. Best of all, we could validate some of these cultures and maybe even learn something from them.

One of the first things other cultures could teach WORMs is that the gospel doesn't have a set dress code. Wouldn't it be nice to get rid of these neckties and Secret Service suits we're so fond of? Contrary to what we've been taught, God cares more about what's in a person's heart than he does about what's on their back.

You don't think so? Well, then how come none of the church's paintings of Jesus show him coming through the clouds dressed like he works for Merrill Lynch?

Imagine attending a sacrament meeting 200 years from now to find a set of log drums being played as a musical number. If you find this objectionable it's mainly because your ancestors didn't worship with drums for 5,000 years, or that you belong to a church started by WASPs whose descendants became WORMs.

What about listening to a Black prophet broadcasting live from Temple Square in Zimbabwe? How about faith-promoting pioneer stories that feature Aztec warriors or Samurai? What if deacons passed the sacrament wearing lava lavas? No way would your Aunt LaVerneece think the church was true then. She'd burn her Tupperware.

I'm also wondering what's going to happen to the church when we hit the Middle East, where the people weren't pressured into giving up plural marriage just because the government was mean to them. How are we going to explain that?

Someone may have to hold the French back, but Mormons generally need more cultural influence. Something needs to help us break out of this stifling WORM stereotype we've confused with the gospel. Different is good.

CRYIN' IN ZION

My neighborhood consists of big Mormon families. There's the Jacobsens across the street with 21 kids, the Rawles with 52 and the Gomezes with 90 and another 140 or so on the way.

These are typical Mo families -- good, honest people who just happen to have reproduced to the point where nature may soon force migratory patterns on them to allow the land to heal.

Ever notice how the more conservative a person's religious beliefs are, the more kids they have? You've got big Catholic families, big Jewish families and really huge Republican families except for, praise the Lord, Pat Buchanan.

This is especially true of Mormons who have, on average, between 4.5 and 37.9 children. The average grows larger the closer you get to Provo where the mini van is widely regarded as the most important revelation since "This is the place."

I don't know how it is for other faiths, but Mormons have big families for a variety of reasons. The most common are:

- Birth control is an attempt to thwart the plan of God.
- Big families are more spiritual.
- "George and I want as many kids as God will send us."

Maybe, but I kind of doubt it. If God really is God, nobody, including Masters & Johnson, thwarts his plans. Also, big families may be more spiritual but you couldn't tell it by sitting near one in church or Burger King. Finally, if you aren't careful, God will keep giving you kids long after your God-given smarts should have said enough.

Talking about having babies is probably going to get me in trouble. After all, there's nothing more sacred to religious fundamentalists than the miracle of life that occurs in a woman's womb. Then again, if you've put 20 kids through it, that's not a womb, it's a bus station.

Although I come from a shamefully small Mormon family of five children, I'm not necessarily against big families. I once asked my dad, an orthodox Mo, why he and Mom didn't have more kids. He said because killing teenagers was a bigger sin than preventing their birth in the first place.

Every family should decide for itself how many children to have. Unless, of course, the parents are the kind of people who shouldn't have kids at all. In which case, the rule seems to be no less than 40 kids in 40 years.

There are ways to avoid having children, most not endorsed by organized religion. There's birth control pills, which are iffy. There's abortion, which is a definite no. And there's the rhythm method, which requires considerable luck, self-control and a math degree to keep track of.

Fundamentalists will tell you that all birth control is bad. So bad that just thinking about sex and not following through with it is a form of birth control.

While to some people it's a sin, my wife and I practice birth control. We have three children, all conceived using a modified rhythm method. We've got a Moody Blues baby, a Crosby, Stills and Nash baby, and a kid we're pretty sure was conceived during a Johnny Cash tune.

Maybe this hurly-burly breeding of the rigidly orthodox is nature's way of ensuring the survival of the species. Think about it. The more inflexible a person becomes about religion, the more obnoxious they are. The more obnoxious they are, the more other people want to kill them. Nature is nothing if not balanced.

HERDING MORMONS

Rebecca Jensen of Holladay wrote a letter asking me to explain Mormon Church structure. Rebecca and her husband recently moved to Utah and are not LDS. Needless to say, they were some confused when neighbors invited them to play "ward ball" at a "steak house."

It's not "steak," Rebecca, it's "stake." Furthermore, it's not "ward ball," but rather "ward brawl." If you went, you probably already found that out.

There are two schools of thought on how the Mormon use of "stake" originated. One comes from a time when a large group of Mormons were standing around on the prairie. In order to make sense out of this mess, stakes were pounded in the ground. People were then told (commanded) to go stand by such-and-such stake and be counted (unto).

The second origin is less likely and refers to the stakes that Native Americans sometimes tied Mormon pioneers to preparatory to a game called "Fun with Ants."

Stakes are comprised of anywhere between five and a dozen wards. A stake periodically holds a conference during which all wards meet in the same building. Because of ward boundaries and the basic ironies of Mo life, this is sometimes the only opportunity Mos have to talk to other Mos who live right across the street from them.

So there you have it. "Stake" has nothing to do with "steak" or any other kind of beef, unless, of course, you're talking about cramming 3,000 Mos in a building for stake conference. Then there's a definite herd factor involved.

At the risk of confusing you further, here's a fast run-through of other Mormon organizations.

WARD -- This is the basic Mormon unit of people measurement. The geography of a ward is based on Mormon population density. In Utah, a ward covers about three blocks. In Mongolia, about 4,000 miles, and then it isn't a ward but rather a "branch."

REGION -- While a bunch of wards is a stake, a bunch of stakes is a region. For the average Mo, a region serves no purpose except when it comes to basketball championships.

AREA -- Your average Mo hasn't got the slightest idea how much ground or how many people an "area" covers. All I personally know is that I've been to a couple of "area conferences" in my time. Secretly, some Mormons believe that "area" was a euphemism for "family" during the days when the church practiced polygamy.

MISSION -- While most consist of foreign countries, there are no set requirements for mission size. The church sets them up wherever there's a need to reach large groups of people who may or may not be ignorant of the gospel of Jesus Christ. Like Utah.

QUORUM -- Wards themselves are divided up into various sub-organizations. For example, it's a "quorum" of elders, a "group" of high priests, a "society" of women, a "gaggle" of geese, and so on. There's also a "troop" of Boy Scouts and a "nursery" of kids, although there is a movement underway to have this changed to a "shriek" of kids.

SYMPOSIUM -- As in the annual Sunstone "symposium." Unlike other Mormon organizations, a symposium doesn't have set number of people. It's anytime two or more free-thinking Mormons get together and say stuff not heard in Sunday School.

Known scripturally as "secret combinations," all symposiums are frowned on unless they are ordered and operated by the church, at which time they become a "Fireside."

KNOW JACK ABOUT MORMONS

Having been one myself, I feel amply qualified to write about jack-Mormons.

Most newcomers to Utah arrive thinking that Mormons are all the same. The truth is substantially and even pleasantly different. There are some Mos who act more like no-Mos than Mos. The vast majority of these are jack-Mormons.

Most people, including most Mormons, don't know jack about jack-Mormons. Hence, our lesson for today. First, a brief jack-Mo history.

A long time ago, the term "jack-Mormon" was used to describe gentiles who sided with Mormons on such things as lifestyle, politics and annoying the federal government. Eventually, jack-Mormon actually came to mean the exact opposite -- a Mo who has sided with gentiles on such things as lifestyle and politics and making the bishop nuts.

Today's jack-Mormon usually doesn't attend church. He or she may drink coffee and alcohol. They might even smoke tobacco and other more pagan stuff. Jack-Mos are not always married to their significant other and they're not locked into a one party political system.

Jack-Mormon isn't just a Mo phenomenon. Other churches also have words to describe the less than ardent members of their faiths. The few that come immediately to mind are "backslider," lapsed believer," and "that guy we're going to burn to death in morning."

If you want to get picky about it (and many today do), there is a politically correct way to refer to jack-Mormons. Regular Mos call them "inactive members", although the current buzzword is "less active members." Both refer to the Mormon in question being a non-practitioner of the faith. The closest non-Mormon example I can think of is a Republican who voted for Ross Perot.

Point of caution: Mormons who have deliberately parted company with the church are not jack-Mormons. They're ex-Mos. The difference between the two is subtle but definable. Whereas a jack-Mo can be indifferent or even friendly toward the church, an ex-Mo has usually found a new ax to grind and is itching for the chance to try it out on a few Mo necks.

A good litmus test for telling whether you're dealing with a jack-Mo or an ex-Mo is to ask them about the Mormon faith. The jack-Mormon will normally shrug and say, "Beats the hell out of me, buddy." Conversely, the ex-Mo will go off on some tangent every bit as fervent and wearisome as a testimony meeting.

I'd be careful with this, though. Ask that question to the wrong Mo and the missionaries might pitch a tent in your yard.

It's also important to note here that being a jack Mormon doesn't mean you're automatically a jack Utahn. Many jack-Mos have deep ancestral roots in this state and will be just as incensed as a Mormon when it comes to Utah bashing. In fact, your odds of getting punched in the head for a derogatory comment about Utah is significantly higher with a jack-Mormon.

Jack-Mormons typically make good friends for both Mos and no-Mos. For no-Mos, the jack-Mo is a non-threatening (albeit somewhat inaccurate) source of information about the church and Utah.

Despite their differences, Mos have a lot in common with jack-Mos. Better still, the jack-Mo won't automatically rat you out to the bishop for not behaving yourself.

DARE TO BE PREPARED

If all religions had to choose an animal to be like, Mormons would probably be squirrels. I make this assertion after having cleaned out the storage room in our basement where we keep our church mandated "two year supply" of food.

Next to white shirts, politics conservative enough to make Idi Amin nervous, and a passion for goofy multi-level marketing plans, the hallmark of a Mormon is food storage. For years now, our leaders have counseled us to lay aside a supply of food for the tough times ahead.

Squirreling away food for a rainy day is probably a good idea even for non-Mormons. Only someone with unwavering faith in the federal government could possibly believe that things are always going to be as they are. And since having unwavering faith in the federal government is akin to worshipping Satan, Mormons store food.

The purpose of food storage is to be able to live for a certain amount of time without going to the store. The ideal is anywhere from a year to two years. The real is, on average, about eight hours. If we didn't need hair spray and TV Guide, my family could hold out for maybe 30 minutes.

While Mormons are counseled to be diverse and smart about our food storage, the typical Mormon's food storage is probably a lot like mine. In my basement, I've got 14 tons of wheat, two cans of unidentifiable preserves, a box of matches, 200 back issues of the Ensign, a tourniquet and a big can of honey.

The tough part about food storage is that it's heavy and it goes bad. Not bad so much in the sense of spoilage (although it does that too) but bad in the sense that it develops an attitude, a literal mind of its own.

I've got plastic bottles of emergency water with pre-Cambrian life forms wiggling around in them. One of the 55-gallon drums of wheat must have gotten wet because the barrel has bulged into the shape of Joe Waldholtz, and neither I, nor the Army Corps of Engineers has the guts to take the lid off. The honey is so old that it's turned into a 50-pound Jolly Rancher.

Worse, if your food storage isn't going bad, it's just going. That's because when a Mormon moves, he takes his food storage with him. Anyone who has done this rarely does it twice, mainly because a bag of wheat weighs more than a Wells Fargo safe.

A neighbor once insisted that our elders quorum help load 800 plastic soda pop bottles filled with water into a Ryder truck. It was part of his food storage and therefore sacred. So there was no convincing him that he should pour the water out and refill the bottles once he got to his new home. At least there wasn't until the quorum got into some serious laying on of hands around his neck.

Preparing for tough times isn't just a Mormon thing. More and more people are starting to worry about the future. Those that aren't storing food are building compounds and baiting the government.

I asked a no-Mo friend of mine what he was doing to prepare. Turns out that he has a food storage plan, too, although he didn't get it from the Ensign magazine. He got his from Soldier of Fortune. His two-year supply is an M-16, 30,000 rounds of ammunition, and whatever is stored in my basement.

CRUISING FOR CHRIST

Last week, I got an advertisement in the mail inviting me to participate in the 1996 Christian Tours Program. For 3,000 bucks, I could "feast my eyes and feed my soul" by vacationing with other true believers on "wholesome" gospel oriented cruises.

NOTE: These tours are only open to people who want to avoid the more traditional hedonist tours where people actually cruise for Satan.

Among other things, the Christian Tours Program wants me to enjoy the spiritual experiences of "cruising for Christ" to Caribbean islands where there are "tales of swashbuckling pirates and buried treasures" and "romantic, sun-kissed beaches."

My guess is that these were wholesome Errol Flynn-type pirates, not your real gap-toothed and smelly pirates who slaughtered people for fun and profit. Also, the sun-kissed beaches that Christian tours go to were never graced by naked, sexually attractive savages like Bo Derek, but rather modestly attired island inhabitants like Gilligan and Mrs. Howell.

An additional irony in the brochure was the fact that the average cruise for Christ costs about what it would take to feed an Ethiopian village for a year or put Bibles in every motel room in Texas. Aboard the luxurious H.M.S. Sunday School, you'll be able to eat yourself sick, listen to gospel music, and have a romantic (but clean) time, all within hailing distance of some of the worst poverty on earth. Haven't these people ever heard of Jonah?

Alas, I can't do it. Not because I'm above that, but rather because I don't have 3,000 bucks. If I did, I wouldn't spend it on a Christian cruise. I'd spend it on the cruise I see on television, the one where Kathy Lee Gifford is cavorting about in a bikini the size of an

American Express Card. Actually, my wife says I'd spend it on a garage.

I don't know, a gospel vacation sounds to me like yet another Christian marketing attempt to simultaneously serve God and Mammon. Granted, it's not as spiritually tacky as, oh, say a Las Vegas wedding chapel/pawn shop, but it comes pretty close.

The closest I've ever come to a "wholesome" Christian tour was my mission. It cost a gob of money, lasted for two years and included ports of call in places so exotic that Christians were still considered delicacies. Worse, my fellow travelers were some of the most uptight people in the universe. The last thing I want to do for a rollicking good time now is do it all over again.

Generic Christians aren't the only ones getting in on the gospel tours scene. I've also received advertisments for "Book of Mormon tours" to Central America where I can "walk the paths that ancient Mormon prophets trod." For upwards of 2,000 bucks (plus local bribes), I can participate in this "unforgettable gospel experience." No thanks. Forty years of Sunday School has been unforgettable enough.

When I go on vacation, I'm trying to escape the irritating routines of my life, one of which happens to be church. Before you bust a corset stay, I'm not saying that church isn't necessary, just that it isn't necessary for a wholesome or even spiritual time on vacation.

It's possible to be spiritual on vacation without cruising for Christ. Most of my life's top ten spiritual experiences occurred while on vacation, and none of them while sitting in church.

Let's see, there was the sun rising over the Grand Canyon, tide pools on the Olympic coast, and morning mist over the jungle falls of Iguazu in Paraguay. Oh, and having my bags searched by Bolivian customs officials. If that doesn't put the fear of God into you, nothing will.

Best of all, none of these cost 3,000 bucks.

BOYS TO MEN-TAL

Even though I was a Boy Scout, I never got my Eagle. As a Mormon male, that's sort of like admitting that you didn't go on a mission. People around here don't quite know what to say when a guy admits to a lack of interest in the outdoor part of the gospel plan.

When I quit, the ward scoutmaster said it was probably for the best, that some boys didn't do well in an overly-structured environment (unless maybe it was prison). My father said second class was higher than any Kirby had ever gone in Scouting and I should quit before maybe it went to my head.

Although some people would like to see a separation of church and scout, the truth is: I learned a lot about Christianity during my scouting days. There's nothing quite like being 14 years old and 200 miles away from his folks to make a guy realize that the struggle between good and evil is not only interesting, but downright cool.

In the summer of '67, our ward scoutmaster Ray Buckwaller, crammed 13 boys into his camper, padlocked the tailgate against the door, and drove 400 miles without stopping. It was a two-week lesson in gospel truths.

I know what you're thinking, that this is going to be one of those Reader's Digest stories where, in some outdoorsy epiphany, a boy becomes a man. Not even.

See, while Mormons like to think their kids are a cut above other kids, you only have to take them camping to learn that Mormon kids are in fact no different from other kids, which is to say a gang of mentally-impaired Huns.

The first gospel thing I learned on that scouting trip was never to go with the crowd, especially if the crowd believes that it can become drunk on a large bottle of vegetable oil. An hour later, there were several horrible accidents in the back of Ray's camper. Despite our frantic pounding, Ray wouldn't stop. Which in turn taught me a lot about long-suffering.

The gift of tongues was a valuable lesson that summer. I learned it in part from fellow scouters, but mostly from Ray when he blew a tire near Richfield, got out to fix it, and discovered what had happened in his camper.

I learned even more when we got to the lake. Some stuff about knots, swimming and getting lost, but mostly about eating dirt-covered meat and going to the bathroom in the weeds -- two things which served me well later in the mission field.

Scouting taught me to be respectful of authority. This I learned from listening to a forest ranger scream at Ray after Harold Price and I chopped a tree down across the highway.

I also learned respect for all God's creatures, but mainly for skunks after we tried to catch one with Ray's sleeping bag.

Perhaps the best gospel lesson, however, was the one about pleading for forgiveness. This Ray demonstrated to perfection after Harold and I tossed a "fish grenade" into the tent of a neighboring camper considerably larger than Ray.

Ray made me ride up front with him the entire way home. That's when I learned that it's OK for grown men to cry and even become hysterical. Years later, I heard that Ray was awarded the Silver Rodent.

I wouldn't swear to it in church, but I'm pretty sure that scoutmasters like Ray go straight to heaven, too.

FASTER FAST SUNDAYS

People unfamiliar with Mormon Sunday worship mistakenly believe that we only have two kinds of Sundays. There's General Conference Sunday, which polarizes Mormons between Temple Square and Lake Powell.

Then there's regular Sunday, which takes about 80 percent of the population of any Utah community and crams it into a ward house for three hours.

The truth is that Mormons are much more diverse than that. Once a month, we have something called Fast Sunday. Fast Sunday differs from other Mormon Sundays in two ways.

Way #1 -- Mormons aren't supposed to eat anything from Saturday evening until after church on Sunday.

Way #2 -- Regular sacrament meeting is given over to testimony meeting wherein ward members get up and say what's on their mind.

When I was a kid, the term Fast Sunday confused me. If it was fast, how come it went so damn slow? Hey, when you're 10 years old, starving to death, and forced to listen to someone blather on about the gospel, time loses all meaning. Back then, I knew adults long-winded enough to make the sun stand still.

Fasting, of course, means that you go without food for a time. For Mormons, the purpose is to save the price of the meals skipped and donate the money to help the needy. On Fast Sundays, Mormon boys come around and collect the money for the ward. Makes sense when you think about it.

Mormons fast in a variety of ways. Most go without eating actual food and water for the prescribed time period. Others believe that literally nothing should enter their mouths during that same time.

While I personally don't think that gum is anti-fast, I've seen hungry kids stare at me in testimony meeting.

"How come Brother Kirby is chewing gum on Fast Sunday?"

"Because Brother Kirby got it from Satan. Do you want gum from Satan, hmm?"

For you more orthodox fasters, I'd like to point out that Listerine is not only a good idea socially, but it won't break a person's fast either. If you can't trust your own common sense here, check with your bishop.

Now that I'm an adult, I find the testimony meeting part of Fast Sunday more tolerable. Usually it's the same old stuff: adults testifying that they're grateful for this and that, or a string of about 30 kids who repeat the same thing verbatim.

But every once in a while, when you least expect it, someone will depart from the norm. They'll get up and testify to something that would turn Geraldo Rivera's hair white. It doesn't happen very often, but enough to keep me coming back.

That's not to say that Fast Sunday is always bad. When I was a cop, I could rack up my entire monthly ticket quota by running radar on Fast Sundays. I'd just park between a ward house and a subdivision where lots of hungry Mormons lived. It was like an airport.

It was also risky business. When it comes to general unreasonableness among a religious group, bomb-toting Middle Eastern terrorists have nothing on your average Fast Sunday Mormon headed home with a ham sandwich on his mind.

Important technology has also been discovered because of Fast Sunday. Most people don't know this, but Ab Jenkins, who sped to world fame on the Bonneville Salt Flats in 1940 while driving a car dubbed the "Mormon Meteor," was just trying to get home from church on a Fast Sunday.

WEIRD – THEM OR US?

ESPN interviewed me when they came to town in March. Unlike "60 Minutes," ESPN's interview was hardball. They wanted to know why Utahns are so darn nice to their sports teams? They thought it was because Utahns are mostly Mormons and Mormons are mostly nice.

I told them the truth, which is that Mormons are family oriented. That means we don't care about NBA stuff as much as we do our kids. And if you call a foul on our kid in a ward or high school ball game, we'll kill you.

When the piece aired last week, ESPN left the "truth" part out. Instead, they had me saying something innocuous like "Utah sports fans don't misbehave because we're afraid of going to hell."

The same thing happened to President Gordon B. Hinckley during his recent "60 Minutes" interview. He too said something that viewers may have taken out of context.

"We're not a weird people," President Hinckley told Mike Wallace.

When I heard that, I almost lost my testimony. However, after giving it some more thought, I came to the conclusion that what President Hinckley really meant was that Mormons aren't any weirder than anybody else. Which, if you think about it, is a far cry from saying that we're weird-free.

CAUTION: I hesitate putting words in the prophet's mouth, mainly because I'm not very smart, but also because I don't want to go blind, turn into a leper, or get called into the ward nursery. So please forget I said anything.

The truth is that Mormons ARE weird. But as weird as we are, we have never:

- Eaten anyone.
- Communed with space creatures.
- Held ward parties to celebrate the Simpson verdict.

If you follow the national news at all, this doesn't even come close to putting Mormons in the category of weird as defined by the Federal Agency in Charge of Who's Nuts in America. Frankly, anyone who thinks Mormons are the weirdest bunch of people they've ever seen doesn't get around much.

I once had a friend tell me in the same breath that Mormons were bizarre and that she was a Druid. Is that a scream or what? Two weeks ago, I overheard a Baptist minister denouncing Mormons for steadfastly believing that they alone were right about God, something I guess Baptists never do.

More recently, I attended a party and listened to some guy harangue Mormons for their opposition to gays. Could there be, he demanded, a more homophobic place in the world than Utah? I mentioned Mississippi, Saudi Arabia, Uruguay, Guatemala, Texas, Iran, the Freeman Compound, my grandma's house, the Vatican, until he told me to shut up.

My personal favorite irony, however, was a feminist who, five seconds after declaring all men pigs, called me a sexist simply because I was a Mormon. How's that for weird?

The truth is that the entire human race (including and maybe even especially you) is one great big collection of idiot savants. Each and every one of us is fair-to-medium smart about one or two things and a complete goof about everything else. As such, obsessive behavior and idiotic tangents are the hallmarks of being human. It also explains why no group of people larger than two has any business looking down its nose at another.

If "60 Minutes" really wants a story, they should pick a group of people at random (like maybe your family or mine) and look for the weird.

DRESSING LIKE A MORMON GUY

A while back, I was in the church office building trying to get to the roof to take a picture of the top of angel Moroni's head for a Sunstone article. I mean he looks gold from the street but you never know. He could really be a brunette.

On the way up, the elevator stopped several times to let people on. Three, to be exact. All were thirty-something men wearing dark suits, white shirts, neck ties, and sensible shoes. I asked them if they were related.

When you see guys dressed like that, it's not hard to peg them. Your choices are pretty much limited to Mormon/ insurance/ Republican/all three.

If you're new to Utah, I know what you're thinking. "Kirb, how can I dress like a Mormon guy?" That's okay. Everyone wants to fit in with the crowd.

First, you're not going to look like a Mormon guy if you just go out and buy a dark suit and a white shirt. Mainly because this is also the preferred dress of inexpensive lawyers, secret service agents, Nation of Islam bouncers, and Denny's restaurant managers. It's more the subtle things that define male Mormon fashion.

For starters, you'll need a tie tack, something that discreetly proclaims your inner self and keeps your tie from hanging in casseroles at ward eats. Most LDS males opt for a miniature of the Salt Lake temple, angel Moroni, Eagle Scout award or a paper clip

The most original tie tack I've ever seen on a Mormon was in a photograph of Apostle J. Golden Kimball. His tie tack was a molar. Incidentally, this is the only Mormon fashion trend ever started by a general authority that failed to catch on.

This logically brings us to the subject of ties. Mormons get their neck lanyards from one of three places: a relative's closet, K-Mart, or Christmas. The tie should be reverent, at least ten years out of fashion, and contain no more than 25% red material. It should also be sturdy. You never know when you might need it to strap a 5-year-old kid to a pew.

Current (and eternal) Mormon trends dictate black, gray, blue, or really dark brown suits, all cut in a style referred to by the gentile fashion industry as "ecclesiastical bulk."

While it is possible to get away with a western cut sport coat, pin stripes or even a blazer, never try to pass yourself off as a

Mormon guy while wearing a red suit. I once saw a guy in a russet-colored number chased out of church and down the street by a group of Mormons who thought he was the devil.

Who makes the suit isn't important, although Mr. Mac, Sears and grandma are quite popular. Mormons are more conscious of price than they are brand names. "Two for one" means more to us than Armani, who, if asked, most Mormons would say was a Book of Mormon prophet.

Next up are shoes. Gucci is out (see Armani reference). So are Birkenstocks and Bass Weejuns. As a rule, Mormon guys prefer to be shod as if they were about to cross the plains again. Wing tips or mailman shoes are big. Combat boots may be allowed in some Montana wards, but definitely nothing two-toned or with tassels.

It's easier than it sounds. Start out slow and gradually blend in. For about $39.95, no one will ever be able to tell that you aren't a Mormon guy.

GOSPEL BLACK BELTS

Last week, there was a story in the Religion section about Catholic nuns learning karate. It seems that nuns over in India -- a country known for its greater tolerance of livestock than religious differences -- are being harassed by hoodlums.

The nuns at St. Anne's convent near Madras take a 45-day course to learn how to counter knife-wielding thugs and to throw jabs at throats and groins. They even let a jeep roll over their hands to toughen them up.

By the end of the course, the nuns say they feel bolder, stronger and more self-reliant. They went right out and signed on as extras in the soon to be released "Nun Chucks IV."

Their instructor, Shihan Husaini, claimed the nuns were better students than the soldiers he has trained. "At the end of it, I'm sure that no hooligan in a lonely street will be able to harass them," Husaini said.

I've got news for Shihan. Hooligans don't think that way. I spent 11 years carrying a gun, a nightstick, Mace and a surly inclination to use them. Hooligans still harassed me.

Furthermore, there's this jeep business. If it toughens up the hands, how come running over their butts with a jeep hasn't caught on among women concerned about cellulite?

OK, I'll stop. The truth is, I'm jealous. When I went on a mission, nobody taught me anything about self-defense. All I got was some memorized Spanish and a ticket to a place full of people who, if they didn't actually hate Americans, wouldn't have necessarily cared if we got torn to pieces either.

In addition to the normal allotment of drunks, lunatics and bugs the size of construction equipment, the country where I labored also contained an alarming number of communists. Sometimes, when worked into a real political snit, the commies came after us.

When that happened, my companion and I never resorted to martial arts. We always turned the other cheek. Referring, of course, to the ones on our behinds. We harkened unto the spirit and ran like electrified pigs.

Still, it would have been cool to know karate back then. Instead of running away, I could have backed the commies down with a fine display of Christian karate prowess. A few flying kicks here, a shattered knee there and we could have gotten down to the business of learning charity and love. Instead, the government rounded all the commies up and shot them.

The problem with gospel karate isn't knowing how to use it as much as it is when. That's probably why my church doesn't teach karate to missionaries. It's hard enough to get missionaries to use the scriptures prudently, much less something that could hurt people.

"For the discussion on forgiveness, Brother Kramp, I think we'll use the Horse, the Crane and maybe even the pulling out of a heart."

I'm also glad that other religions never got into the martial arts. One night when I was a rowdy teen, some friends and I were indulging in a bit of brainless vandalism behind the Holladay Community Church when the pastor caught us.

Instead of smashing my clavicle with a Whirling Cross-Eyed Monkey Punch, the pastor gave us all a lecture on good citizenship. I remember that it was a message of brotherhood and love even though he had a handful of my hair at the time.

Christianity just wouldn't be the same today if Jesus had been a black belt.

VISIT TO THE ENEMY

My wife and I ditched church last Sunday. It left us cranky and out of sorts. It's our own fault. That's what happens when you miss your nap.

Actually, we went to church. Just not our own. We attended the Evangelical Free Church in Orem. Pastor Scott McKinney is an acquaintance of ours, and, more importantly, a guy with some skill at preaching. I didn't even get drowsy.

When we told some of our Mo neighbors that we were going to the Evangelical Free Church, their response was both predictable and interesting.

"Aren't those the people with electric guitars and snakes?"

I said I didn't think so. The truth, however, was that we hadn't really known Pastor McKinney all that long. He could have been a snake handler and a Jesus screamer. I'm all for finding ways to stay awake in church but I draw the line at snakes.

When you walk into another faith's church, there's always this feeling of entering an enemy camp. The people there don't believe the same way you do, ergo they've got to be dangerous, right? All you really know about them is what you've heard, which is a pretty narrow if not downright stupid way of judging people.

The Evangelical Free Church wasn't like an enemy camp. Sure things were different, but a good different. Best of all, no snakes.

There was, however, a guitar. In a Mormon church, we sing our hymns accompanied by either a regulation piano or organ. Mormons consider it irreverent to use anything else including bagpipes, nose flutes, zithers, tubas or really irritated cats.

The guitar worked for me. Even though I glimpsed something of an ex-rock and roller in Bob Cash, the man playing it, his music was so reverent and beautiful that I experienced something I haven't felt in years: the urge to sing a hymn without first being struck in the head by a hymnal.

Following the music, the Evangelicals celebrated high school graduation by awarding Bibles to the graduates. The kids testified about how important it was to them to have found God, which I thought was great even though they didn't find him my way. At their age, I was more interested in finding a place to hide from the police.

Then came Pastor McKinney's sermon. Whereas the word "evangelical" may bring to mind a Bible-thumping television preacher with a diamond pinkie ring and a pending federal indictment, Scott is none of that. He dresses simply, preaches calmly and doesn't take American Express.

As a Mormon, I should have found a lot of doctrinal nits to pick in Scott's sermon but I couldn't. His was a common sense Christian message about the importance of putting God in charge of our lives because, frankly, we aren't smart enough to be our own bosses. It made perfect sense to me and so I said "amen" along with everyone else.

Worshipping with the Evangelicals was great even though we're "supposed" to be enemies. The way Christianity seems to work these days, Scott should exclude me because I'm a Mormon and therefore not a real Christian. Conversely, I'm supposed to ignore Scott because not only is he not a Mormon, he isn't even in my ward.

Although I had to ditch my own, I learned something by going to Scott's church. You might want to try it yourself because when Jesus returns, he'll probably have a lot to say about how xenophobic we've all become in his name.

MORMON KITSCH & GRAVEN IMAGES

Two weeks ago, the bishop's son brought me a golf ball with the Salt Lake temple embossed on it. I've got a large collection of Mormon doo-dads and kitch, but no temple golf ball. My guess is that it was intended to be a spiritually guided golf ball.

Didn't work. Cody, the kid who found it on the back nine of the Hobble Creek Golf Course, said the shooter hooked it about 900 yards in the direction of Manti. Most LDS theologians agree that there are only two possible explanations: somebody was either playing on Sunday or the ball got its temples confused.

There may be a third explanation. Putting a temple on a golf ball appears to be in direct violation of the graven images commandment. If it is, God probably doesn't like it. And nobody can mess with your swing like God.

The graven image possibility is a legitimate concern for Mormons these days. Heretofore, we've looked down our noses at other faiths' infatuation with shrines, idols, crosses, and fish-shaped bumper emblems. The truth is we're getting in on the act ourselves.

The cross is the primary symbol of faith for some Christians. Although Mormons don't subscribe to the crucifix as a religious image, we havc developed some graven images of our own. Like the cross, the sight of these images is intended to bolster our faith and make a gob of money for the people marketing them.

Today, some of the most prominent images or symbols of LDS worship are the "Y," Angel Moroni, Mormon vanity license plates, bread machines, and Steve Young posters and/or actual Steve Young shrines.

But the most prominent LDS graven image is the CTR ring. The letters stand for "choose the right," although strong argument is occasionally made for "choose the Republican" and "conversion through repetition."

Like crucifixes, CTR rings come in various styles, from the basic silver 'member" ring at $11.95 all the way up to the 14k gold "calling and election made sure" ring at $169.95. There's even talk of a CTR ring with an actual sliver of the Nauvoo temple in it.

Typically, CTR rings are worn on fingers. However, I once spotted a CTR ring in the nostril of a guy with greasy hair and facial tattoos.

Except maybe when BYU plays the University of the Underworld, Mormons don't pray to their CTR rings. They're to remind the wearers to behave in times of crisis such as first dates, tax audits, and R-rated movies. Proof that they work is the fact that Mormons haven't had a repeat of Mountain Meadows.

However, it should be noted that CTR rings have not been proven effective against vampires.

Whether it's wearing a cross or a CTR ring, I can't fault anyone for symbolizing their faith with a religious image. As long as it makes them behave like something other than an imp of Satan, who cares?

Still, I may have been a little hard on the owner of the temple golf ball. Upon closer inspection, it appears the ball was intended as a gag-wedding gift. I don't need a solid gold CTR ring to tell me what I should do with it. Finders-keepers is definitely not the CTR way.

If anyone knows Dave and Gina, married Aug. 8, 1995, in the Salt Lake Temple, tell them I've got their golf ball.

THE ONE AND ONLY TRUE CALIBER

In Utah, the holy hub-bub these days seems to be whether or not you can shoot somebody in church.

Wait a minute, that's not right. OK, whether or not you can shoot someone in church if they deserve to be shot. Hmm? No, that's not it either.

How about this: Whether or not Jesus would help you reload if you had to shoot more than one person in church?

Forget it. We'll never resolve the issue as long as it's a stupid one.

For the record, I'm against carrying concealed guns to church. Not because it's a totally bad idea, but rather because it can be a huge pain in the ass. Particularly if the gun goes off when you hadn't planned on it.

I should probably point out here that I carried a concealed Colt .45-caliber Combat Commander to church for eleven years. I did it because small town cops are never off-duty. No matter where you go, including church, people don't stop seeing you as a cop.

That's not necessarily a bad thing unless, of course, a guaranteed bad thing happens. If it does, people invariably say, "You're a c-c-cop. D-do something."

Whenever that happened to me, I usually preferred having a gun inside my jacket rather than a Book of Mormon. Not that the book is bad, but it didn't do much for Joseph and Hyrum at Carthage. Then again, neither did the concealed pistol they had.

Take it from me, the cons of packing heat in church far outweigh the pros. You don't know what a contrite spirit is until you've cracked a Sunday School kid in the head with the butt of a gun. About that time I switched from a belt to a shoulder holster.

Even though writing religion columns is more dangerous than being a cop, I no longer carry a gun to church. That doesn't mean that I don't sometimes wish I still did.

Just last week, I found myself wondering how many shots it would take to make Brother Guffer shut up so we could have the closing prayer and go home. In fact, I'll bet all church speakers would think twice about droning on if they knew the audience was not only annoyed but armed.

But like other facets of religion, I can see the issue of guns in church going to the extreme. It wouldn't be long before zipper covers for the scriptures started coming with holsters. Eventually there would even be bitter inter-faith disputes over which caliber was God's true caliber.

Also, for Christians, there's the inescapable irony of carrying a gun into a meeting where the main idea is to worship the Prince of Peace. If you can't see that irony, chances are pretty good that you shouldn't be carrying a gun much less be allowed to go to the bathroom by yourself.

I probably wouldn't be so down on the idea of guns in church if I had a better view of people in church. Despite a 2,000-year-old commandment to love one another, we're still using religion as an excuse to alienate each other. Given this level of smarts, it's a wonder that God lets us have driver licenses much less concealed weapon permits.

Over all, packing guns into church is a bad idea. Mainly because history has proven that when it comes to human beings, religion is a dangerous enough weapon all by itself.

CLOCKING THE SECOND COMING

Years ago, I had a missionary companion who believed that the Second Coming was so close we wouldn't even finish our missions. Elder Karpas claimed Jesus was going to arrive in all his glory sometime within the next few months.

"I can't wait," Karpas would say. "All the wicked will be burned as stubble."

Karpas studied the scriptures diligently for the signs of the times. Sometimes he got up on the roof of our apartment to see what color the moon was. So cranked on the Second Coming was Karpas, that he occasionally scared our converts bad enough to make them cry. One of them even took a swing at us.

Whenever he got too wound up on the Second Coming, I'd ask Karpas if he thought we had time for lunch or a haircut before Jesus came. Irreverent comments like that always made him mad.

"Light-minded people will get fried when the Savior comes," he said.

After about three months of this nonsense, I volunteered to give Karpas a preview of the Second Coming courtesy of a broken neck. Instead, he got transferred to Monja Muerta where he was watching for the signs of the times so hard one day that he got hit by a produce truck.

That was back in 1974, and, since Jesus isn't here yet, it's pretty obvious that Karpas was either wrong or an idiot. Because he also claimed that prayer worked better on mosquitoes than insect repellent, strong argument exists for both.

Christians have been penciling the Second Coming into their daily planners for 2,000 years now and nothing has happened. We're still waiting like it's going to be tomorrow at 1:36 p.m. for sure. If not, it'll be the day after tomorrow for sure.

Every year, some yahoo predicts Christ is going to return on a certain day. They've got it all figured out based on stars, scriptures, educated guesses and talk shows. But every time someone gets it down to a day, the day arrives and no Second Coming. Even though some people think it's a sin, the Idaho lottery gives better odds.

I think it's a little harder to read God's mind than that. Somebody trying to predict the movements of God is like a really stupid gopher trying to program a VCR. Frankly, people didn't even get it right the first time Jesus came. Most of them couldn't even figure out who He was.

Don't get me wrong. I believe in the Second Coming. However, as a practical Christian, I don't know when it will come.

The card-carrying Christian cynic in me takes it a step further. I say that anyone who claims to know even approximately when Jesus will come should be shot with a tranquilizer gun and safely removed to a remote area.

Too many Christians view the Second Coming as the arrival of a SWAT team. Jesus is going to roast sinners when he shows up. Hoping for the Second Coming like that reduces Christ to the level of the Boogey Man. "Be good or Jesus will get you" tends to defeat the purpose of having a Savior in the first place.

It seems to me that all this energy spent studying the signs of the time really ought to go into learning how to recognize Jesus when he finally does arrive. Remember how screwed up we got it the last time?

WAKE ME FOR THE RESURRECTION

On Thursday, I drove my 15-year-old daughter to her early morning drivers ed class. Normally my wife takes care of this because the thought of my daughter getting a license fills me with dread. Also because I kill people who wake me up that early.

I had to get up Thursday morning because my wife is out of town. So, at 5:50, my daughter carefully opened the door and threw the cat on me. Waking dad up with a cat is a Kirby family custom designed to keep the person doing the waking from getting hurt. It's hard on the cat, though.

When Whiskers #11 landed on me, I flew into the usual rage. When I couldn't coax Whiskers out from under the bed with a golf club, I gave up and drove my daughter to school. I took solace in the fact that sooner or later I'd be dead and nobody would be able to wake me up.

Then I remembered the Resurrection.

Do you think it'll be that tough to get up on the morning of the Resurrection? I hope not. When the angel blows his horn and 500 billion+ people climb out of the grave, who's going to want to be around if they all wake up cranky? I'll bet that's when lots of people go to hell.

On the other hand, maybe getting resurrected puts you in a better frame of mine. With a perfect body, maybe you won't mind some guy blowing a horn in your ear at 4 a.m. You think? Nah, me neither.

For me, one of the attractive parts about Mormonism is the belief that there are several Resurrections. The one you wake up in is based on how much of a jerk you were during your life. If you have to think about it very hard, chances are that you'll be sleeping late.

It's generally accepted that the people God likes best will get up on the morning of the first Resurrection. Everyone else has to wait their turn.

Herein lies the best reason I can think of for being evil: you don't have to get up right away. Gabriel can blow his horn until his head explodes, and you won't have to get up until it's your turn.

I figure that my wife, Spencer Kimball, Isaiah and Patsy Cline will get up on the morning of the first Resurrection. J. Golden Kimball, Jackie Kennedy, my grandma and John Wayne will get up on the second day. Judas, rap singers and newspaper editors will get up at 9 p.m. on the last day of Resurrection, just in time to catch the last bus to Hell.

Me, I plan on getting up whenever I feel like it. After all this time on earth, I'm fed up with other people telling me when to wake up. My idea of paradise is being able to sleep as late as I want. What's the point of a heavenly reward if it comes with reveille?

Then again, when God says get up, you get up. It's something I learned in the Army. If a drill sergeant throws a fit because you didn't wake up on time, just think what God would do. Remember Sodom and Gomorrah, hmm?

Maybe I better play it safe. If you're in the ground near me when the horn goes, give me a nudge. Better yet, there should be plenty of cats around. I'll get up in a few minutes.

THE PRODIGAL BUMS

The last time I saw Bammer was the spring of '71. To this day, I can't hear "Layla" by Derek & the Dominoes without thinking of him, a '65 Dodge and a hookah pipe in the shape of Richard Nixon's head. In fact, that's all I remember from 1971.

Devoted followers of Timothy Leary, Bammer and I hung out in Sugar House Park where we thought we were the coolest things happening. In reality, we were just a couple of skinny, wired creeps with more hair than brains and the life expectancy of a couple of bugs.

I thought Bammer was dead. Someone told me that he overdosed in '75. So, needless to say, I was bit shocked when I came face to face with Bammer in the Cottonwood Mall last month.

Sitting in the American Grill, I glanced over at the next table and there was Bammer's old man eating some pasta. Except that I had been to Mr. Wilcox's funeral and knew for sure that he was dead. I must have stared too long because the woman with Bammer finally nudged him and pointed at me.

"Kirb?" Bammer said, stunned. "I thought you were dead."

We spent the next two hours catching up. We were amazed to discover that we had both cleaned ourselves up by getting religion. This, despite considerable pressure and harassment from friends -- some of whom really are dead.

You might claim that maturity rather than religion is what really sparks the desire to change. In our case, however, it was the police. One night, God bless 'em, the Salt Lake County Sheriff's Department fell on Bammer and me like the Philistines.

Getting yanked through a car window and dragged off by my hair was a pivotal point in my life. I started looking for a new direction. I found it two years later while going door-to-door in a South American slum.

Bammer's stabilizing influence was a girl who made him get a job, go to church and have a Zig-Zag Man tattoo removed before she agreed to sleep with him via eternal marriage. He's a guidance counselor in Idaho now where he also teaches early morning seminary.

There's a point to this story. Namely that Bammer and I have spent years trying to repent of our evil past by forgiving and forgetting. Forgiving ourselves was the easier of the two. But despite years of effort, neither of us have been able to forget that we were once in league with the devil.

No matter how much you try, you never really live down your past. The best you can hope for is that you'll be able to live with it. That and maybe that your kids won't find out. It's tough to set rules as a parent if your kids know that you used to get loaded and talk to park ducks.

I think the reason people can't forget bad stuff is because God doesn't want us to. After all, being able to remember what a low-life you once were helps keep you from becoming one again. Better still, you just might be able to point out hazards to other erstwhile low-lifes.

Forgiving yourself is cool, but I don't think it's a good idea to forget. You just might forget the price you paid to get where you are. Worse, you might start taking for granted the sacrifice someone else made to help you get there. And I don't mean Timothy Leary.

PREACHING TO THE FAITHLESS

A few weeks ago, I spoke at the First Unitarian Church. Hey, they invited me.

Driving up to Salt Lake, I couldn't help thinking about the irony. Not so much that the Unitarians had invited a Mormon to speak, but rather that they were so casual about it. My own church makes me take a polygraph exam before letting me get anywhere near a pulpit.

I think the talk went rather well. Nobody told me that I was stupid for being a Mormon and I came home with all my arms and legs. When it comes to religion these days, you can't get much better than that.

A number of things impressed me about the Unitarians. First was that they tended to be more intellectually nimble than the people I normally sit with in Sunday School. That means a lot to a guy who once fell asleep in church during his own talk.

Second, there was a question and answer period after I got done speaking, an important element long missing from LDS meetings. It would put a whole new spin on fast and testimony meeting.

"Sister Barrage, can we go back to the part about how your cancer got cured by 100 percent Homemaking meeting attendance?"

The Unitarian questions were direct but non-punishing. They wanted to know why I go to church if I hate it so much, when will LDS women get the priesthood, and why isn't Steve Young married? As best I can remember, my answers were:

- I hate vegetables too but they're good for me.
- Don't know, don't care.

- Shoot, if I had 40 million bucks and women mailing me their underwear, I wouldn't get married either.

The absolute guaranteed best part about Unitarians is that they're a come-as-you-are crowd. Even though it was Sunday, I only saw one neck tie in the congregation; and it was on some guy wearing a T-shirt.

The Unitarians almost had me there. I mean that I came this close to converting. I don't know about you, but the thought of attending church in shorts and sandals is a very compelling theological argument.

Mormons have a stricter church dress code. Still, unless you happen to be a missionary or an employee of BYU, it's nothing etched in granite.

Typically, Mormons are expected (mostly by other Mormons) to show up in church wearing their Sunday best. Generally speaking, we believe that Jesus only wants you for a sunbeam if you're wearing a J.C. Penney suit or a nice floral print dress. And no cross-dressing, either.

The usual Mormon churchwear taboos are makeup on guys, pants on women and SCUBA gear on anyone. The idea is to keep things tasteful while worshipping God. That's also why deacons aren't allowed to wear earrings while passing the sacrament.

Although it may sound hypocritical, I agree. While I may want to wear sneakers and jeans to church myself, when it comes to religious ordinances, I prefer to have them administered by someone who doesn't look like they're trying out for a bit part in an Al Pacino flick.

Then again, it's a little easier for me to take someone seriously if I know they aren't just following the pack. A general authority getting up in conference wearing a Jazz T-shirt would definitely hold my attention until the next station break.

It might be his last day on the job but I'll bet he'd say something interesting.

NAME CALLING IN GOD'S NAME

Last week, Russian security leader Alexander Lebed called Mormons "filth and mold." Lebed's comment made a lot of very important Mormons mad, among them Utah senators Orrin Hatch and Bob Bennett, and my mom.

I too thought Lebed was out of line. What does he really know about Mormons? He hasn't even started taking the discussions yet. If he's that mad at the church now, just wait until he has to start home teaching and paying tithing.

The human thing to do would be to respond to Lebed with something equally nasty and derogatory. I say we call Tom Barberi on a mission to Russia. After all, if anyplace in the world needs someone to make fun of the government's attitude toward booze, it's got to be Russia.

What shouldn't happen is for Mormons to get all bent out of shape because Lebed called us names. Toward that end, I hereby denounce the motion made in priesthood quorum meeting last week to brand Lebed a "gentile-Commie-fat-head."

While it has never been official LDS policy to refer to other people as "mold," "scum," "filth" or even "nasal discharge," we have called them names in the past.

Remember when we called the Catholic church the "great and abominable?" That was pretty bad. In terms of impoliteness, it's way worse to call somebody's church the "mother of harlots" than just plain old "filth."

How about when we called everyone but us "gentiles?" That certainly wasn't very nice. It wasn't very original, either. We stole "gentile" from the Jews, who, incidentally, Lebed also doesn't like very much.

"Mold and filth" isn't something I take personally. Maybe because I've made a hobby out of collecting the bad names that people have called me by mail. My personal favorite to date is "you modern-day Korihor," although "Mormon [expletive deleted]" comes in a close second.

When you get right down to it, the word Mormon was originally a derogatory name. We didn't start out calling ourselves "Mormons." We thought of ourselves as "saints."

It was other people who started the "Mormon" bit. As in, "Them damn Mormons are at it agin, Virgil." Say "Mormon" like Lebed would say "mold and filth" and there you have it. Now say Missiourian the way you would "mold and filth" -- well, OK, never mind.

Still, it's not surprising that people don't like being called names. Maybe that's because names are sometimes the precursor to even worse stuff. In high school, "#@&! was usually a warning that your nose was about to change size and shape.

It's worse coming from a government leader. "Filth" is probably the last thing somebody like Lebed might think before pulling the trigger on a gun he'd just wedged in your ear. He strikes me as a guy big on sticks and stones.

What is surprising about religious name-calling is that some people today are shying away from names that used to be flattering. Like, oh, "Christian."

It's true. According to a recent news story, some Christians don't like to being referred to as Christian anymore. They say that instead of Jesus and love, the word "Christian" conjures images of intolerant moral extremists and/or whore-chasing television evangelists.

Jesus doesn't go for name-calling. This despite the fact that He indulged in it a little bit, himself. Remember when the Savior called us a "generation of vipers?" Now that hurt. Probably because there's a good chance that it's true.

INBREEDING THE RIGHTEOUS

Mormons and members of other religious sects frequently refer to each other as "brother" and "sister." If you subscribe to the idea that God is our father, it follows that we're all his children and therefore related.

When I go to church, it's always "Sing, Brother Kirby" or "Wake up, Brother Kirby." Almost nobody calls me by my real name or even something really bad. At home, my neighbors say stuff like, "I'm calling the police on you, Brother Kirby."

I've read pioneer journals where wives and husbands called each other "brother" and "sister." My favorite is, "And then Brother Pitchfitz said to me, 'Sister Pitchfitz, is it not now time to get thee with another child?'" With a line like that, my hope is that she said "nay."

Referring to each other as brother and sister is supposed to remind us that we're all part of the same big family. We're supposed to love and support one another, be there for each other.

Reality is a bit different. The behavior of the average family begs an important theological question. Namely, does centuries of brothers and sisters marrying each other explain why there are so many idiots in the world today?

While a few less renowned religious scholars may disagree, I say that it does. Science has proved that you can't muck around with the gene pool like that or your kids will end up with buckteeth and heads the size of golf balls.

Religion has proved it as well. If you don't think so, read the Old Testament. Everyone in it acts like God gave their brains a quick stir before he sent them down here. The movie "Deliverance" could have been a screen adaptation of parts of the Old Testament.

We could, I suppose, blame it all on Adam and Eve. We might not be in this fix if our original parents hadn't been brother and sister. But what choice did they have? Not only were they the only two people around, God told them to get busy and have kids. And a few years later, their kids were killing each other.

Then again, maybe this kind of behavior is the way God planned it. When He gave Adam and Eve the boot from the Garden, God told them that life was going to get way tougher. Why blame it all on the devil when simple inbreeding could explain a lot of it?

Families are supposed to be nice. "Families are forever" is even a popular Mormon refrain, most of whom view it as a wonderful perk for behaving. More practical Mormons wonder if it isn't also a threat. Who wants to spend eternity with kids, especially if they're related just a bit too close for their own good?

Yesterday, one of my daughters tried to shove her sister's head in the toilet during an argument over a hair brush. My wife/sister came home and wanted to know why I didn't stop it. I said it was a sign of hope. If our daughter/sister wasn't actually trying to kill her sister/sister a la Caine and Able, maybe the gene pool is trying to straighten itself out.

The larger world family behaves the same way. Entire nations bicker over trifles exactly like siblings. It makes you wonder why the United Nations doesn't have a pickup, four hound dogs and a banjo playing moron in the front yard.

UNSPIRITUAL AWAKENING

I'm frequently asked how I stay awake in church. The answer, of course, is I don't. What's good enough for the top priesthood echelons is good enough for me.

When I was kid, sleeping in church as a means of coping with boredom wasn't an option. The natural state of my six-year-old bio-rhythms coupled with the five Ding Dongs I ate before church made sitting still about as likely as an angelic visit.

Growing up, I was a master pew squirmer. Squirming is the only way a kid who normally expends 8,000 calories an hour careening around the neighborhood like he was on fire can cope with something like church.

For those of you who don't know or have forgotten, squirming is done mostly with your butt. An average pew squirmer can move around pretty good on just his behind. A master pew squirmer, however, could dance Westside Story using just his hams.

Pew squirming makes parents mad. "Try paying attention," is what they say to squirming kids, which makes about as much sense to a kid as "Try breathing through your belly button." It can't be done.

Besides, even a kid knows that if church was interesting enough to pay attention to, more adults would go. And the ones that did go wouldn't fall asleep, let their minds wander, or think up reasons to be excused.

Years ago, my wife started paying me a dollar every time I stayed awake through an entire sacrament meeting. As of last Sunday, she owes me 458 bucks. How did I do it? Easy. I thought up ways to make sacrament more interesting.

Before we get into them, you need to understand that when it comes to church, there's a big difference between "can't" and "not supposed to." Some of the things I'm about to suggest won't be found in the Ensign magazine. They might even make you (and others) uncomfortable, but they won't get you thrown in jail, at least not in and of themselves.

They will, however, keep you awake, and that's the whole point. I mean how're you going to get to heaven if you can't stay awake in church? So that makes anything that keeps you awake in church good, right? OK, not drugs, but anything else.

Here they are then, Brother Kirby's Top 10 Ways to Make Sacrament Meeting More Interesting (as previously given at Sunstone):

#10 -- Pass a note along the pews to the Relief Society president asking her to meet you at a hotel tomorrow. Sign the bishop's name to it.

#9 -- During the musical number, hold a Bic lighter aloft or crowd surf toward the podium. Bring Frisbees and beach balls to toss during the warm-up act (prelude music).

#8 -- During an exceptionally boring talk, imagine the bishopric a) making gagging motions behind the speaker's back, or b) in drag.

#7 -- Show up at church dressed in a militia uniform, a Satan costume, or in drag yourself. Be sure to sit up front.

#6 -- Snap your fingers and call "Waiter!" during the sacrament. Leave a tip.

#5 -- Applaud, boo or rebut testimonies as the occasion requires.

#4 -- When a father holds a baby up following a blessing, make hog calling noises.

#3 -- Pretend polygamy has been reinstated and mentally select three women from the congregation to be your new wives.

#2 -- Tell your wife who the new wives are.

#1 -- Let your wife pick the three new wives.

DRIVING SUNDAY CRAZY

I took a drive with my family on Sunday. We went up over the Nebo Loop and down into Nephi. In some places on the back of Mt. Nebo, the leaves are already turning.

Perhaps the best part of our family drive was that we left two of our three kids at home. All in all, it was a pleasant, if unholy, Sunday drive.

That's right, unholy. Several years ago, I read in an LDS priesthood manual that taking the traditional Utah Sunday drive with your family was not conducive to keeping the Sabbath day holy.

At the time, I wasn't the spiritual beacon to the world that I am today. I wrestled with the matter, wondering what could possibly be more holy than spending quality time with your family in a confined space? Especially if you leave most of them home.

I'm older and wiser now. I've got enough Sunday driving experience under my belt to testify to the evilness of Sunday drives.

A number of things detract from the spirit during a Sunday drive, not the least of which is that no matter where you want to go on your peaceful jaunt, it's a sure bet that everyone else in the world had exactly the same idea ten minutes before you.

Three years ago, my family did the Alpine Loop on an autumn Sabbath. I left home a mild-mannered Mormon father and came home a slavering homicidal fiend. Which, as you might expect, is way bad for the spirit.

Proof that Sunday drives are bad for your testimony is that God allowed some idiot to invent the Winnebago. There's something about following one of these waddling $40,000 port-a-potties up 30 miles of switchbacks that just makes the spirit descend the hell all over you.

You may have started out looking for leaves and deer, but get stuck behind a motor home and all you'll end up looking at is retirement bumper stickers. Before I do the Alpine Loop again on a Sunday, I'm going to get me a bumper sticker for the front of my car. "You may be spending your kids' inheritance today, pal, but who's going to spend your life insurance tomorrow?"

It's not just motor homes either. Drive up any canyon in Utah on a Sunday and it's gospel that you'll encounter the slowest driver on earth. Either it's tourists gawking at deer or it's some guy two days older than dry land who can't figure out what all that honking behind him has to do with who spilled cocoa on his sleeping bag during the blizzard of '38.

Then there's Sunday driving death. Two years ago, I accidentally hit a potgut near Strawberry. The way my girls sobbed and wailed during the rest of the drive, you'd have thought I ran over Brad Pitt.

Finally, there's ice cream cones. Your chances of getting killed by a drunk driver on Sunday are nowhere near your chances of getting blasted by some guy trying to drive a landing craft full of kids and lick a double-dipper at the same time. On Sunday, I came around a bend and nearly went head-on with a mini-van in my lane. The miss was so close that we got splattered with Rocky Road.

Want my spiritual advice? Stay home on Sunday. Even if you take drugs and watch bad movies, you'll be safer and closer to the spirit.

MORMON PORCH APPLE

The story goes like this: A visitor to Salt Lake City is being shown around by a Mormon. The sight-seeing trip includes the state capitol, Temple Square, the Delta Center, and Karl Malone's house. After noticing that his host never locks the car, the visitor asks why.

"The crime rate in Utah is really low," the host explains. "So we don't bother with locks."

On Sunday, the two attend church at a local ward. Getting out of the car, the visitor sees his host taking elaborate precautions in locking the car. The Mormon notices the visitor's surprise.

"If we don't lock the doors," the Mormon says, "the car will be full of zucchini when we come out."

Whether or not this story is true, it serves to illustrate a well-known and bizarre LDS attraction to a species of summer squash.

For those unfamiliar with zucchini, the squash -- also known as the "Mormon watermelon" and the "Mormon porch apple" -- is bright green and not bad tasting when cooked with equal parts butter, salt and wooster sauce.

Zucchini comes in three sizes. Small is anything under the size of a silkworm missile. Medium ranges up to the size of an Airstream motor home. Large is everything else including a zucchini so big that it will actually usher in the Apocalypse.

Utah's affinity for zucchini began years ago when Mormons were counseled by church leaders to grow gardens as a mean of remaining self-sufficient. Zucchini quickly became the star attraction of Mormon gardens because even the most inept gardener could grow it. You can't kill zucchini with napalm.

Because zucchini grew so well, there always seemed to be a surplus. Soon began the LDS custom (now gospel ordinance) of sharing zucchini with neighbors. Called "Laying off the Zuke," so devout is the approach to this solemn principle that today 99 percent of all zucchini grown in Utah are grown as gifts.

Zucchini is also an important LDS missionary tool. Newcomers to Utah cannot consider themselves officially welcomed to the state until they've found zucchini on their porch. If the zucchini comes in the form of zucchini bread, you'll know that you've been targeted for baptism. That, or a Church calling.

In some parts of Utah, zucchini isn't just a Mormon thing anymore. As Utah becomes more mainstream, so does the hardy Mormon squash. I've been to artsy parties near the University of Utah where people smoked dried zucchini. A real zuke high reportedly enables them to "see" their family genealogy clear back to Adam and Eve.

Two months ago, I went to an Olympic celebration dinner where zucchini daiquiris were served as a cute way of toasting Utah. Nobody got drunk. In fact, the more they drank, the more conservative everyone became. Five drinks and Bo Gritz became the new Messiah.

But these are examples of zucchini adulterated. The truth is, zucchini is a Mormon vegetable. It's every bit as much of an LDS trademark as hand carts, white shirts, the Osmonds, and corporate fraud.

Fundamentalist Mormons actually believe zucchini got its name from Zucchini (pronounced zoo-key-nigh), a little-known Book of Mormon prophet who lived in Zarahemla, led a people called the Zuchites, and made an obscene amount of ziff from his insurance sideline.

Practical Mormons like me are the anti-Zuchites. We don't grow, cook or eat zucchini, and we believe that zucchini is really just a Latin word meaning "garden tumor."

SQUARE MORMONS

General conference is over for another six months. Interestingly enough, that's almost exactly how long it takes for harried Salt Lake City traffic cops to start believing in God again.

Like Catholics, Jews, military juntas and Republicans, Mormons are happiest only when they're in big groups. That's why there's been an LDS general conference (pronounced "gin-rel con-ferns" south of Point of the Mountain) almost as long as there have been Mormons.

The first conference was very small. It probably only consisted of Brigham Young yelling at some people from the back of a wagon. But not long after the Saints settled in Salt Lake City, conference became the special cheek-to-jowl event we have now.

Visitors and newcomers to Salt Lake City think every Mormon in the world gets dressed up on the first weekend of every April and October and heads down to Temple Square. Not true. There's no way all 9 million+ Mormons could fit in the Tabernacle. It just seems that crowded when you're trying to find a parking spot at Dee's.

The truth is that most Mormons stay home for conference. They're known as Home Conference Mormons (HCMs), to distinguish them from the more pious Square Conference Mormons (SCMs). The only way to tell the two groups apart during the rest of the year is that SCMs get a lot of testimony meeting mileage out of actually having been there.

Most Utahns are HCMs of a necessity. For example, it's not really feasible for Mormons in Bolivia or Angola to attend conference. So they stay home and listen to conference while wringing a chicken's neck for dinner, pounding on their radios for better reception, and wishing they were on Temple Square.

Conversely, Utah HCMs stay home and watch conference on big screen TVs, perfectly happy that they aren't downtown where the traffic is bad enough to drive a seminary teacher to diet Coke. It isn't fair but what are you going to do?

To varying degrees, HCMs regard conference weekend as a "get out of church free" pass. Free meaning that there's none of the guilt normally associated with not paralyzing your butt in a three hour Sunday meeting block. HCMs know they can mow the lawn, work on their cars and even party during conference because stake presidents and bishops are mostly SCMs and far away.

Of course, HCMs aren't all the same. Like Mormons in general, they come in varying shapes, types and compulsions. Because you rarely see an HCM in action -- most of the media coverage is hogged by SCMs -- perhaps it's time we examined them.

Conservative HCMs take home conferencing very seriously. They'll put on their church clothes, set up folding chairs in the living room and watch conference as if they were right there in the Tabernacle. When there's a station break, they sing hymns and pray.

Moderate HCMs gather the family together and watch conference in casual attire. Sometimes they discuss the importance of the talks during station breaks. Occasionally, Dad falls asleep.

Liberal HCMs watch conference in their pajamas while eating salsa and chips. During the station breaks and choir songs, they sometimes play Nintendo. Or so I have observed at my house.

Radical HCMs tape conference and may watch it when they back from Lake Powell where, oddly enough, the traffic is also bad during general conference.

WANTED: LAWYER FOR THE JUDGMENT BAR

Ever since O.J. Simpson got off, I've been thinking a lot about the Judgment Bar. See, I've allegedly committed a lot of sins. I say allegedly because these sins haven't exactly been proven in court yet. And maybe they never will be. You don't know.

Mostly, I've been wondering if I'll be allowed a lawyer when it comes time for me to be judged before God. There's nowhere in the Scriptures that says I'm entitled to counsel, but then it doesn't say I'm not, either. It's best to be prepared.

If I am entitled to counsel, I don't want some cheapo public defender. No way. When it comes time to defend me against charges of alleged sinning, I want a real lawyer. I want a lawyer like O.J. got, one that costs at least $5 million and knows how to schmooze the media.

See, the tough part of the Judgment Bar is that we aren't going to be judged by a jury of our peers. Frankly, I wouldn't be that worried if we were. After watching the Menendez, Simpson, and L.A. police trials, I'm guessing that creating a reasonable doubt in the minds of a jury is the intellectual equivalent of shining headlights on deer.

Nope, we're going to be judged by God. And word is that God's a little tougher to confuse than a jury. That's why I figure that I need a lawyer. A good lawyer -- one with a Mercedes.

God isn't going to be like Judge Ito, either. Try saying "I object" to God and what you'll get in response is an immediate legal decision known as Blast Furnace vs. Snowflake. God takes no guff and nothing under advisement.

God also doesn't let you stand before the Judgment Bar and say weenie stuff like "I wish to assert my Fifth Amendment privileges." Mainly because He knew what the evidence was even before you did.

The evidence against me is pretty bad. I've never killed anyone, although I have on occasion really wanted to, mainly on I-15 around 90th South during rush hour. Oh, and one time while stuck in a room with a guy who liked Rush Limbaugh.

I've never committed adultery except occasionally in my heart with KUTV's Mary Nickles. God and my wife may say it's the same thing but you can bet that Mary doesn't. I certainly don't.

The most expensive thing I ever stole was a Tommy James and the Shondells record in 1968. Most recently, however, I've coveted my neighbor's Bayliner. Also his truck, motorcycle, hot tub, snow blower and paycheck.

I worshipped idols once. But it was at a Fleetwood Mac concert and I've since repented.

As you can see, things are looking pretty bleak. The way things stand right now, it'll take God about .0003 seconds to return a verdict on me. The sooner I find a lawyer, the better.

The trouble is that all the good ones are busy. O.J.s lawyers are so hot right now they're probably already being booked by Hitler, Genghis Kahn and the creators of "Baywatch." Even if they aren't, I don't have the money to hire them. Johnny Cochran spends more on dry cleaning than I make in a year.

My mom says she'll defend me for nothing. She says that when it comes to understanding a person's true nature, only God could know and judge them better than their own mother.

I'm in a lot of trouble.

BLASTING OF THE DEER

Dawn today marked the beginning of the high holy days in Utah. Even as you read these words, hundreds of thousands of worshippers are in the mountains celebrating the annual manhood rite known as the Blasting of the Deer.

Known as "deer huh-in" by its less sophisticated devotees, Blasting of the Deer is a sacred rite among Utahns, one that transcends all denominational boundaries. As such, it probably shouldn't be mocked.

What the heck. The only people who might object are shivering around a campfire above the tree line right now, some of whom won't be found until next year. Lets have some fun.

Actually, this is serious stuff. Over the years, I've made a study of the Blasting of the Deer. Indeed, there was a time when I participated in the rite. This occurred long ago when I truly believed that Nirvana could only be reached by turning one of God's prettiest creatures into jerky and dog food.

I fell from grace the way most Blasters fall. I got married to a woman who had a testimony that meat costing $652 a pound wasn't much of a bargain, spiritual or otherwise. I know, I know, filthy lucre got me like it got Judas, but there it is.

Here in Utah, Blasting worshippers come in two distinct denominations: Gentile Blasters and Mormon Blasters. Actually, there's a third group, more pagan in its theology and practices. They are the much despised "@&*! California Blasters."

The devotions of Gentile Blasters are pretty straightforward. On the eve of the rite, they make a pilgrimage into the mountains, sometimes sobbing and on their bellies, but usually in Jeeps and trucks. They pitch camp and proceed to feast, make merry and fire the symbols of their priesthood at the moon. In the morning, they arise with big heads, blast a deer (more often not) and return home spiritually edified.

Mormon Blasting of the Deer is much more complicated than that. Primarily because Mormon blasters only have 24 hours to celebrate the Blasting of the Deer before they're legally supposed to be back in church.

Among Mormon Blasters, the Sunday following Blasting Day is known as "Cursed Sabbath," a day when they either return to their lowland wards or remain, riddled with guilt (among other things), in the mountains. Cursed Sabbath is not to be confused with Super Bowl Sabbath, another highly unpopular Mormon Sunday.

So zealous are some Mormons in their Blasting faith that they have even crossed over to become Gentile Blasters, even if it's just for the duration of the Blast. Fallen from the purer faith, they can be found participating in Gentile Blasting rituals, most notably the sacred rite of the Bellowing Intoxicant.

It's a tough choice when you have to choose between two forms of worship. And Mormon Blasters have not always chosen wisely. The Blasting of the Deer has almost become a genetic factor among many of us.

It's rumored, but not yet proven, that in some LDS wards a young man can't get out of the Aaronic Priesthood until he's killed a deer with a can opener. An electric one. Poaching is grounds for excommunication.

Mormon church history experts say that the Blasting of the Deer is where some LDS feminists stake their claims to the priesthood. So strong is the call of the mountains to men during this time, that women have had to take over for them on Cursed Sabbath.

THE SACRAMATING GAME

About five minutes after the Mormon church got started, my ancestors joined up. They went through all the initiatory rites to be Mormons in the old days: whippings, burnings, mobbings and really, really long meetings.

Eventually, along came the big Mormon trial -- polygamy. My ancestors participated in that, too, although probably not very successfully. Kirby isn't exactly a common Mormon name and none of us are general authorities.

While none of my relatives are polygamists now, I have a few friends who are. I asked one of them what benefit there could possibly be in having more than one wife. John said it taught him great humility.

I told John he was an idiot. The average male gets sufficiently humbled from being married to only one woman. Anyone who needs six wives to humble him has got to be a slow learner with a bullet-proof ego.

Even though the LDS church abandoned the practice, lots of Mormons claim that polygamy is still God's plan and that we'll be living it again some day. I hope not. Right now, my marriage is at least a fair fight. There's only one of my wife and one of me. When my wife and I don't agree on something, there's no way she can gang up on me.

Still, my wife and I are Mormons and so we try to stay in practice for the big day. We do this by playing a little sacrament meeting game we call "Choose the Wife." The game assumes that all the women in the ward are husbandless and we've been "called" to choose three of them as new wives.

Even though it's only pretend, Choose the Wife can get pretty heated. It's earned me at least one hymnal up the side of my head. But it usually doesn't come to that because there are strict rules. Actually, there's only one rule. The rule is that my wife and I have to agree on who the wives will be. This explains why we've never actually played a round of Choose the Wife all the way to the end.

Because the choice is limited to the women in our ward, there's no way I can pick Kim Bassinger or Pam Anderson to be my new wives. I can live with that because there's also no way my wife can stick me with Whoopi Goldberg or Felix Urioste.

Choose the Wife goes something like this: I pick Sisters X, Y and Z as our new wives. In turn, my wife chooses Sisters A, B and C. Then we begin negotiating. It's the negotiating that makes me realize I would have made a lousy polygamist.

My wife invariably claims that I pick Sisters X,Y and Z because they're slim and attractive. Conversely, I argue that Sisters A, B and C are gruff and demanding, each weighing about as much as a fully loaded Buick.

Contrary to what my wife believes, Sisters X,Y and Z aren't chosen for their looks, but rather for the looks of their husbands. It's probably cheating, but I figure that if Brothers X,Y and Z seem content and happy, I stand a good chance of being treated well, too.

My wife says polygamy isn't fair and won't be until we can play "Choose the Husband." Fine by me. While there aren't many women in our ward that I'd want to marry, there are a lot of men I'd like to see get whacked in the head with a hymnal.

HOME TEACHING IN THE LAST DAYS

My home teachers showed up on Halloween like they do every year. Being the official last day of the month, Halloween is unofficially also home teaching day in the LDS church.

This year, my home teachers, Ray and Al, were dressed as the Blues Brothers, which I thought was apropos. Mission from God and all that stuff. I gave them some Smarties. Cheap, I know, but I don't waste Baby Ruths on people just doing their jobs.

"We're just checking in," Ray/Elwood said while peering around my front room for beer and crucifixes. "You're still gainfully employed and alive? Need anything?"

"Yes, yes and no."

For the benefit of you non-Mos, home teaching is an LDS church program whereby the priesthood gets out once a month and visits every member of the ward to see how they're doing. Two men are assigned the responsibility of home-teaching two or three families each month. Being non-Mos, you don't have to worry about this. Your big concern are the missionaries.

Officially, home teachers are supposed to come in, sit down, offer a spiritual thought and say a prayer. They're supposed to become your friends so that you'll rely on them in times of need. It works. Al and Ray fixed my VCR once.

As bothersome as it might sound, the idea behind home teaching is a good one. You never know when someone in the ward will need help, especially if they don't get around so good.

For example, if you've got an elderly widow in your ward, it's a pretty good idea if someone checks to make sure the heat's on and that the cats haven't eaten her. If you can learn to genuinely care about her, that's even better (besides being the whole point).

Most Mormon men function as home teachers. Most Mormon men also prefer to home teach active families. The reason being that church-going families are, for the most part, low maintenance. They know and play by all the home teaching rules. Sometimes they'll even feed you.

Inactive families are harder to home teach. They require exhorting and inspiring to do things you might not be all that keen on yourself, like going to church. Inactive families can be pretty hostile, too. But the rules say you have to keep trying until a) they become your best friends or b) it takes a police hostage negotiation team to save your life.

Personally, I never fail to do my home teaching. It just seems like it. That's because some months I do covert home teaching. Undercover home teaching means that I do my home teaching but no one (including the families themselves) knows that I do. They have to take my word for it because it's classified.

Home teaching can seem pretty pointless. Case in point, I home teach two of my neighbors, people I see every day of my life.

Our lives are so intertwined that sometimes I know before they do that they're going to get fired/sick/audited/divorced/shot.

Home teaching isn't just a Mormon male thing. The women do it, too. It's called visiting teaching (referred to in priesthood quorums as visiting screeching) and accomplishes the exact same thing. It's also done on the last day of the month.

Our visiting teachers for October were Thelma and Louise.

WHERE'S MY HEALING FEELING

You'll have to forgive me if I ramble. I'm in a lot of pain right now, both physically and spiritually. I had a hernia operation last week and it shook my faith.

A couple of months ago, I developed a small abdominal bulge where no bulge had previously existed. It kept getting bigger. After some debate -- my wife said tumor while I said alien -- I went to the doctor. His diagnosis was an operation that today closely resembles the aftermath of an armed robbery gone wrong. I quietly gave up a bunch of money to a man in a mask but got shot/stabbed anyway.

None of that matters anymore, thanks to my new friend Perk O'Dan. What has shaken my faith through all of this, however, are the stories in the Bible about sick people being healed via the miraculous power of prayer and religious rites.

I've been a Christian my entire life and whenever I've gotten really hurt or sick, it's always taken a nagging wife, a doctor and more money than I make in a year to fix me up. Not once have I been made whole again because of a miracle. And frankly, I'm getting a little fed up.

Before you run off in a religious snit, I'm not saying that God doesn't heal people. I believe He does. He's just always healing other people -- people in the Bible, the Ensign and the Watchtower. Never me.

I grew up on faith-promoting stories of Jesus healing the sick, casting out demons and raising the dead. It wasn't just Jesus, either. His apostles also got in on the act. Pretty soon lots of people were doing it.

Even today some people rely on blessings to get better, calling modern medicine a crutch of the faithless. Some extreme faiths will actually let people die rather than have a doctor administer to them. I know fellow Mormons who think the priesthood is a catchall replacement for surgery, Midol and even Rogaine.

Never mind, I'm not talking about religious loonys. I'm talking about me, your average common-sense believer. Where's my faith healing? How come I'm always getting stuck with an HMO instead of a less expensive miracle?

My qualifications are certainly all in order. While I've never been possessed or been a leper that I know of, I have been darn sick. I had double pneumonia during my mission and nobody showed up to heal me. In fact, my companion left me to die in our apartment while he went back out to work with a local elder because our monthly stats were low.

The only person who came by to comfort me during this difficult time was the Trix rabbit, although a doctor later said this was a hallucination brought on by high fever coupled with the normal sensory deprivation of mission life.

In addition to disease, I've been in car wrecks, fights, falls, industrial accidents, misunderstandings with big animals and even a medium-size explosion. Never have I looked up through a fog of pain and found an apostle ready to make me whole again.

All of this might have made me bitter but I started thinking that maybe I'm being saved for something special. Maybe God is storing up the miracles due me so that when I die, I'll get them all in a lump sum in the form of being raised from the dead. Yeah, that's got to be it.

Let's see an HMO beat that.

BEEFY MORMONS AND WoW

One of the first things most gentiles learn about Mormons is that we don't smoke or drink. Or at least we're not supposed to. It's called the Word of Wisdom and it was the first attempt at establishing an HMO in Utah.

Established more than a century ago, the Word of Wisdom today is interpreted as a strict ban on smoking, drinking and coffeeing. Most people don't know that meat is also mentioned in the WoW as something that should be eaten "sparingly" -- translated by many Mormons to mean no more than 12 pounds at a single sitting.

Eating lots of meat isn't a strict WoW item but it probably ought to be. After all, other things have become hard and fast WoW rules without being mentioned at all. Crack cocaine, airplane glue, acrylic paints, and large caliber gunshot wounds.

Coke and Pepsi aren't mentioned in the WoW but have become to really staunch Mormons the spiritual equivalent of heroin and maybe even cold-blooded murder.

Another thing not mentioned at all in the WoW but probably should be is body fat. Let's face it, if the whole point of having an ecclesiastically mandated health plan is to stay healthy so you can enjoy life and better serve God, it makes sense not to have a body fat ratio of 312 percent.

Unfortunately, Mormons have been so busy being healthy by not smoking and drinking that we sort of forgot not to get fat. For the most part, we've become a chubby people. One of the great Utah ironies is that of a 250-pound, corn-fed guy in a white shirt and tie looking down his nose at someone having a cigarette.

How Mormons got plump is no secret. When we get together we eat. I mean what else is there? We can't tap a keg or pass out cigars like other people. Ice cream gluttony is what did it to us. Hot fudge sundaes have killed more Mormons than all the mobs in Missouri put together.

Mormons weren't always porky. In fact, our ancestors were a darn lean people. When it comes to staying svelte, there's nothing quite like dragging a load of household furniture across four states and up some big mountains with the federal government hot on your heels. That's probably why you don't see a lot of pictures of fat pioneers.

Historical photos of Brigham Young show him looking kind of chunky. It should be noted, however, that Brigham didn't beef up until after he got to Utah. Face it, if settling down with a wife causes most men to put on weight, think what settling down with 27 wives does to you.

Of course, Mormons aren't the only beefy ones. Catholics have their weight problems, too. So do Presbyterians and Methodists and Jews. But we're the religion so stuck on being healthy that strict adherence to the WoW has become our defining characteristic. If anyone should know better about the dangers of over-eating, it ought to be us.

I'm not saying that Cream o' Weber is the same thing as R.J. Reynolds. Don't be an idiot. But I do suspect that this is more of a temporal issue than a moral one. Frankly, I don't think God is going to kick anyone out of heaven just because they weigh too much or smoke cigarettes. It wouldn't be spiritually correct to discriminate like that.

FISHING FOR THE TRUTH: A BISHOP'S INTERVIEW

My ex-friend new bishop called me up at 4 a.m. and said we were going fishing. He didn't fool me. I knew what he really meant. It was time for another bishop's interview.

A bishop's interview is standard fare in Mormon life. If you want to go to the temple, hold a church position or get permission to vote something other than Republican, periodically you have to make an appointment and go in and talk to your bishop.

Actually, it doesn't even have to be your idea. Do something really stupid -- say kill somebody or attend the Sunstone Symposium -- and the bishop will be calling you. After all, it's his job to see that you're on the right track to a celestial glory.

Most of my bishop interviews have been the usual Mormon spiritual interrogations. That's because all of my bishops have been off-the-rack Mormon authority figures: grim, harried men in suits with conservative haircuts, probing into my personal life like an auditor.

Until recently, the questions were always the same: do I pay my tithing, cheat on my wife, blah, blah, blah, or pray to mother-in-heaven? My answers were equally predictable: Yes, no, I try not to, only if death is imminent, etc.

All of that was before my ex-friend and fishing buddy became my bishop. Things have become less formal since then. My most recent bishop's interview was held in a boat in the middle of freezing Fish Lake with two other guys listening in and snickering.

In a normal bishop's interview, if you don't like what's going on, you can stomp out and call a press conference. Not in a Fish

Lake bishop's interview. Down there, you can leave in a huff and whine to the media only if you can swim fast and hypothermia doesn't kill you first.

"Let's talk, Kirb," Bishop Don Bone said, after we launched the boat and dropped our lines. "How're things going in your life? Are you being chaste?"

"Only by the police," I replied.

But the bishop was serious and wanted to know if I was still lusting in my heart after Sister Mutz. Pooter, who isn't even a Mormon, said he was pretty sure that lusting in your heart wasn't grounds for excommunication and therefore not a legal bishop question.

"Shut up, Poot," the bishop said. Then he asked me if I was paying my tithing and being honest in my dealings with my fellow man.

I said I tried to pay a full tithing so long as it was based on my net income less expenses and court fines, but that it was hard to be completely honest with my fellow man since I figured him to be a collection of mostly morons.

It went on like that through the rest of the interview, me baring my soul while eating frozen Twinkies and cutting up stinking sucker meat for bait. Whenever I hedged on the truth, the bishop (or Poot or Dinger) would correct me because they already knew better.

"Now that's a lie, Bish. I seen him look at a nudie book just last week."

Although it's embarrassing and a little disconcerting, I much prefer the latter bishop interview style to the former. It's probably the one God is going to use at the Judgment Bar because it wastes less time and makes you feel loved and accepted even though you're basically a jerk.

HOPELESS IN THE FAITH

Just the other day, I was asked, "Hey, [expletive deleted], how would like a punch in the head?" This query was followed immediately by a demand to know what I meant when I said some Utahns were "hopelessly Mormon."

I was studying the scriptures in the calm of the Tribune's newsroom, searching for the best way to respond when the spirit dropped a hint. Actually, it was a FAX flung at my head by the editor, but I'm in a faith promoting story mode so bear with me.

The FAX was from John Pitt of Bountiful and Jeff Reed of Ogden and contained a list of hopeless Mormon character traits. When someone comes along with good stuff, I've always been willing to step aside and let their light shine forth. This has more to do with sharing the blame than it does with promoting goodness.

Here goes. You know you're hopelessly Mo if:

"Your explanation for never having spoken to the family right across the street is "What for? They're not even in our stake."

- Your idea of "high class" is fresh flowers woven into the basketball nets at cultural hall wedding receptions.
- You use your calling as a Sunday School gospel doctrine teacher as a forum to present the "Amway Opportunity."
- The school board consults with you personally when forecasting growth at the local elementary school.
- Waitresses automatically add a 15% gratuity when you take your family out to dinner.
- You believe there is spiritual redemption in owning your own wheat grinder.

- You look for the words "Dishwasher Safe" when buying packages of plastic knives and forks.
- You make your children read the Old Testament rather than going to a movie with friends because you don't want them exposed to sex and violence.
- You believe the number "34" has replaced "666" as the mark of the beast.
- You have a BYU cap in the rear window of your car even when you are not driving to Cougar Stadium.
- You can honestly tell the full-time missionaries that you don't know any non-Mormons.
- You see no problem in teaching a Sunday School lesson to a group of boys who saw you punch a referee at a ward basketball game.
- You are anxiously awaiting the "Where Are They Now?" sequel to Saturday's Warrior.
- You can't understand why anyone would pay so much money to see Phantom of the Opera when they can see the stake roadshow for free.
- You think purchases at ZCMI count as Fast Offerings.
- You sincerely believe that family and friends enjoy watching four hours of slides from your church mission to North Dakota.
- Your find it physically impossible to continue facing forward when you hear the over-flow curtain being open in Sacrament meeting.
- You tell your kids that the family vacation money for the entire year was spent on Stake Lagoon Day.
- You insist that your wife and children gather around the TV with you so that you can sleep through General Conference as a family.

For sending in this important cultural research information, Pitt and Reed each received a subscription to National Geographic, lifetime memberships to the Sons of Mosiah (a popular Mormon anti-culture club), and one-on-one meetings with their respective stake presidents.

BROTHER KIRBY...
I WOULDN'T SELL SCAMWAY MULTILEVEL MARKETING PRODUCTS to JUST ANYONE, BUT SINCE WE'RE PART OF the SAME GOSPEL FAMILY...

SQUARING TABS WITH HEAVENLY FATHER

Approximately 2,000 years ago, Mary and Joseph were preparing to be taxed. They loaded everything onto a donkey and went off to Bethlehem for an audit. Everyone knows what happened there instead. It had nothing to do with the IRS, Santa Claus or American Express.

Centuries later, Mormons celebrate the trek Mary and Joseph made to Bethlehem by participating in a ritual known as "tithing settlement."

Along about December, sign-up sheets appear in the foyers of LDS ward houses. Those who want to square their tabs with God, make an appointment to see the bishop. During the meeting, the bishop hands them a list of their financial contributions for the year and asks them if it represents an honest tithing.

However, before we get into that, let me first say that I've got no problem with tithing. When it comes to giving money to God, I tend to agree with a comment made in a 1988 sermon by Reverend Tom Goldsmith of the First Unitarian Church, Salt Lake City. "If you love Jesus, then tithe. Any fool can honk."

The real question is, what exactly constitutes an honest tithing? For Mormons, at least theoretically, an honest tithing is a flat 10% of our income. Actually, it's 10% of our "increase."

The logic here is that you're supposed to show God appreciation for blessing you by giving him back 10% of said blessings. Nothing has ever been said about giving back 10% of God's curses. Mormons believe that tithing helps further God's work here on earth by funding stuff like temples, missions and a football team.

Some Mormons, particularly the orthodoxy, figure tithing based on their gross pay, that is, before taxes. Others pay tithing based on their net income, or what they limp home with after the government gets done with them.

I subscribe to the net plan myself. I figure my responsibility begins once I've got my increase inside my front door. What the wolves ate before I got it there isn't my problem. After all, it's not my job to pay tithing on their increase, too.

Although they are technically an increase, I've never paid tithing on the fish I've caught, spare change I've found, or money won from slot machines, office pools, etc.

Also, unless you've got a remarkably free-thinking bishop, there are no deductions in an LDS tithing settlement, nothing you can write off to lower your titheable income. You can't, for example, deduct the price of BYU season tickets from your tithing. Ditto mileage to church, missionary package postage and subscriptions to church magazines.

Back in the old days, Mormons frequently paid their tithing "in kind." Cash was a rarity, so tithing was brought to the bishop's storehouse in the form of produce or manufactured items.

It went something like this: If you had ten wagon loads of potatoes, how many wagon loads were due the church? Answer: all of them. But most of the time you could get away with just one.

One of my ancestors recorded his tithing in a journal. In 1885, Moriancumer T. Kirby's tithing consisted of, "13 ducks, two pigs, a box of bees, an Indian scalp and a wife."

Personally, I wouldn't mind going back to the old days when tithing was paid in kind. I think it would be kind of cool if in tithing settlement I could just hand the bishop a tenth of everything I've written.

JINGLE BELL ROCKS

One of my friends had a special Christmas experience late the other night. Larry was watching television at home when his son came in from a date and said there were some suspicious looking characters hanging around the bushes outside.

Concerned that it might be thieves or vandals, Larry got up and checked. When he didn't see anything, he went back to the television. A few minutes later, Larry's daughter called from her bedroom and said she saw a couple of shadows scurry up the driveway.

Larry checked again and still couldn't see anything. Finally, when he heard someone bump against the garage door, he knew that it was prowlers come to steal. Larry slipped out the back door and gathered up some rocks. Quietly moving to the corner of the house, he peered around it. Sure enough, there were a couple of guys skulking in the bushes near Larry's new truck.

Larry admitted later that he was throwing to kill. His first rock hit one of the prowlers in the head hard enough to drive sparks out of the guy's ears. As additional rocks thudded into them, the prowlers fled shrieking into the night. Larry pursued them, bellowing obscenities and threatening to kill them. Even though he got in some more good solid rock hits, the prowlers still managed to get away.

Returning home, Larry examined his vehicles and property. Everything was fine until he found a ruined fruitcake near the bushes where the prowlers had been lurking. A note on the mashed cake read: "Merry Christmas from your home teachers."

I didn't make this Christmas story up. Right this very minute, there is an ex-home teacher in Utah County with eleven stitches in his head and a really sour attitude about Christmas. Larry feels just awful, although probably not as bad the home teacher. However, all is not lost. Somewhere in the vicinity there are bound to be a couple of happy lawyers.

The moral of this Christmas story is that just because you're operating in a Christmas frame of mind, it doesn't mean that everyone else is. Ergo, spreading Christmas cheer can be a risky proposition.

The proper frame of mind is important if you're going to keep Christmas in it's proper perspective. More than 2,000 years ago, Jesus Christ quietly gave the world the greatest gift possible. No, not a fruit cake, smart-aleck. I'm talking about Salvation.

Over the centuries, the world has come to take Jesus' gift for granted. So much so that today the gift is largely invisible in the glut of materialism that has come to mark the birth of the Savior. We have chased Christ out of our lives with glitter, parties and a selfishness so casual that we don't even recognize it as such. After all, who needs salvation when you've got an American Express Gold Card?

Granted, few people are as mean spirited during Christmas as Scrooge. Most of us have just gotten dull when it comes to why we do what we do at Christmas. Next to Salvation, the greatest Christmas gift is human irony. We're all so busy doing for ourselves that we routinely forget Jesus' message of selflessness.

Give someone a real gift this Christmas, someone you might otherwise ignore. Look them in the eye and tell them that you care about them. You might want to call Larry and let him know that you're coming, first.

Merry Christmas.

PALS WITH THE PUBLICANS

In a few short hours, it's going to be a new year. Rather than bore you with a whole list of possible ways to make your life better, I'm only going to suggest one. It's a resolution for Mormons. Get ready, because it's a doozy.

Repeat after me: "I (your name) do resolve to befriend a gentile in 1996, and to make said gentile an integral part of my life without necessarily trying to convert him.

I'll wait until you stop jumping up and down.

Finished? OK, let's examine the facts. Every year, more and more no-Mos are moving into Utah. You're going to have to make friends with one sooner or later. Why not avoid the Millennium rush and become friends with one now?

Actually, gentile isn't a very good word for a no-Mo. It's just what Mos have called no-Mos for years. It's a word we snitched from the Jews which, translated literally, means "everyone else but us."

Alas, years of Mormon usage has mutated the word "gentile" so that today, the word is synonymous in parts of Utah with "drunkard, lunatic, criminal, Democrat," and "Tom Barberi." Similarly, the word "Mormon" has become synonymous in other parts of Utah with "self-important, tax fraud, narrow-minded" and "Amway representative."

Shake off the stereotypes. Jesus told us to build bridges, not fences. Remember how in the New Testament He drove people nuts by eating with the gentiles and publicans? If it's good enough for the Master, it's good enough for you and me.

That goes for you no-Mos, too. It would do you good to include a Mormon or two on your list of friends in 1996. And no fair getting an excommunicated Mo, or even one who hasn't been to church in 25 years. It's got to be a bonafide church Mo, one with at least two suits.

Admittedly, the idea of being friends with someone other than your own kind is harder for Mos to do than it is for no-Mos. Here in Utah, the LDS church has been in a social rut for so long that most Mormons have a hard time relating to a person who drinks beer, votes anywhere left of Hitler, and readily admits to having read at least one book from the current New York Times best-seller list.

It's actually easier than it seems. As a friend to several no-Mos and even one or two no mo' Mos, let me give you a few tips to help break the ice.

- Do not try and befriend a no-Mo by inviting them to church. They'll think you're being nice just so you can sic the missionaries on them.
- Invite no-Mos to your social functions. Don't get upset if they bring a little wine. Even though it's technically devil's brew, odds are that they won't get blasted and outrage the family dog.
- No-Mos enjoy discussing godless stuff like politics, science and the arts. Conversation ice-breakers that begin with scripture or conference report quotes are not a good idea.
- Be creative. Pretend that the no-Mo is already a Mo, or at least that Jesus wants him for a sunbeam, too. That'll relieve you of the "every member a missionary" responsibility long enough to establish a common ground.

Try and remember that this is for your own good more than it is theirs.

Happy New Year.

THE END

Kirby was born into a military family. After completing high school he served a two-year mission in Uruguay for The Church of Jesus Christ of Latter-day Saints. Upon his return he pursued a career in law enforcement with the Springville, Utah police department (1979). While taking night classes at nearby Brigham Young University Kirby began writing columns for the local newspapers, first the Springville Daily Herald, and later the Utah County Journal (writing under the pen name Officer "Blitz" Kreeg).

In 1989 Kirby decided to leave police work and devote himself to full-time writing. He has written a column for the Salt Lake Tribune since 1994, and has written at least nine books.

Kirby is a popular convention speaker, and travels widely to appear at conventions and meetings. His newspaper columns have won several regional awards.

Kirby presently (2009) lives in Herriman, Utah. He and his wife had three daughters.

Pat Bagley has become an authority on the quirky side of Utah, having served 28 years to life as editorial cartoonist for *The Salt Lake Tribune*. He made a splash nationally with the *Clueless George* series, which has over 50,000 copies in print. Pat is the editorial cartoonist for the Salt Lake Tribune. His daily cartoons have been seen in *Time*, *Newsweek*, *The Wall Street Journal*, *The Los Angeles Times* and over 450 newspapers around the country. He has many books, several of them best-sellers, to his credit which include *I Spy A Nephite*, and the illustrations for *J. Golden Kimball Stories* by James Kimball, as well as numerous works with Robert Kirby. He resides in Salt Lake City.

Made in the USA
Charleston, SC
24 February 2013